Published by Avenue Media Solutions

www.avenuemediasolutions.com

This is Neil Thompson doing what he does best! – taking complex concepts and making them manageable and accessible to practitioners. Don't be mistaken, however; the word 'manual' is not to be taken as a recipe for the neglect of theory or for acquiescing to the status quo – this is a considered text about the nature and complexity of contemporary practice and social work's potential for making a difference. Highly recommended.

Professor Charlotte Williams, RMIT University, Melbourne, Australia

I am very pleased to be able to recommend Neil Thompson's new publication. Neil has a great ability to write and talk about complex issues in an accessible way. Here he draws on his many years of teaching, practising and working with social workers to help us better understand the complexity and richness that is social work. His values, knowledge and communication skills shine through. I thoroughly recommend this manual, not only to students and newly qualified social workers, but also to those with much more experience.

Joe Godden, Professional Officer, British Association of Social Workers

This manual shows Neil's wealth of knowledge and offers a fantastic resource for a broad audience. It is easy to follow, with 'moccasin moments', exercises and reflections. At a time when our profession is stretched and under threat, this reminds us about the breadth of skills, knowledge and values involved; it challenges oversimplification of such core issues as holistic practice, equality, diversity and social justice; and provides a broad range of examples.

Dr Audrey Roulston, Queen's University Belfast

Neil Thompson weaves his vast treasure of knowledge and experience. Why a 'manual' is tackled squarely; it is not a simple 'how to' instruction book which would, as he argues, be simply reductionist. It is a guided illustration of the rich and living tapestry of social work of which we are all part. His practical focus on human relationships, and dealing with difficulties and complexities in a sustainable way is rooted in values. This will become essential reading for social work students.

Professor Jonathan Parker, Bournemouth University

The Social Worker's Practice Manual

By

Neil Thompson

With a Foreword by Professor Mark Doel

Contents

Welcome!

... to The Social Worker's Practice Manual. This manual has been put together to serve as a guide for actual practice. While the theory, the policy and the research are all important and need careful consideration, these are not what this manual is all about. It is about *practice*, about actually getting the job done.

I had so many social work students asking me the question, How do you actually do social work? that I wrote an e-book to answer that question (Thompson, 2016a). Basically, that e-book said that social work is far too complex to be done based on a simple set of instructions – as I have put it so many times: it is not painting by numbers. It is about drawing on your knowledge, skills and values and working out from them what you need to do in each situation (hence the emphasis on reflective practice – see Section 10). I have had a lot of very positive feedback about that e-book, but I have also had people say to me words to the effect that they accept what the e-book says, but they still want more guidance. They know that it would be pointless for me to issue a set of instructions, a sort of recipe book, but they would still welcome more guidance than one short e-book can provide. So, here it is, here is that fuller guidance.

I stick by my claim that trying to do social work in a simple, straightforward formula way is not only doomed to failure, but also positively dangerous. So, what this manual amounts to, then, is a distillation of my experience in social work over a period of almost 40 years. It is the best I can do in offering students and practitioners the benefit of my experience as a practitioner, manager, educator, consultant, expert witness and author over a very long period of time.

It is not a set of easy answers; nor is it a theoretical treatise. In a sense, it is what I would be telling you in supervision if I were your manager; or what I would be saying on a training course if you were a participant. It is, of course, up to you – and your professionalism – what you do with it, but it should provide you with a helpful foundation of what is often referred to as 'practice wisdom'. Use it wisely.

About the author

Neil Thompson is an independent writer, educator and adviser based in Wales. He has held full or honorary professorships at four UK universities. He is a well-published author with over 200 publications to his name, including 39 books, several of which are bestsellers. He has been a speaker at conferences in the UK, Ireland, Italy, Spain, Norway, the Netherlands, Greece, the Czech Republic, Turkey, Hong Kong, India, the United States, Canada and Australia.

He is a Fellow of the Chartered Institute of Personnel and Development, the Higher Education Academy and a Life Fellow of the Royal Society of Arts and the Institute of Welsh Affairs, and a member of the International Work Group on Death, Dying and Bereavement. He was formerly the editor of the US-based international journal, *Illness, Crisis & Loss* and now edits the free e-zine, **THE *humansolutions* BULLETIN**. His main interests are in the field of human relations and well-being, especially: equality and diversity; conflict management; stress; loss, grief and trauma; and reflective practice. He is a sought-after conference speaker, consultant and facilitator.

He has been involved in developing a range of DVDs and e-learning courses for the Avenue Learning Centre. He runs the Avenue Professional Development Programme, an innovative subscription-based online learning community geared towards developing critically reflective practice through supported self-directed learning (www.apdp.org.uk).

He holds a Lifetime Achievement Award from BASW Cymru, the Wales branch of the British Association of Social Workers, and, in 2014, he was presented with the Dr Robert Fulton award for excellence in the field of death, dying and bereavement from the Center for Death Education and Bioethics at the University of Wisconsin-La Crosse.

His personal website and blog are at: www.neilthompson.info. Details of how to connect with him on social media appear towards the end of this manual.

About Avenue Media Solutions

Avenue Media Solutions offers three sets of services:

- *The Avenue Learning Centre*
    - E-books | E-courses | The Avenue Professional Development Programme | Collaborative Learning Programmes | DVDs

- *The Avenue Survey Centre*
    - The Avenue Well-being Survey – are you getting the best out of your staff? | Health and Safety – are you doing your best to protect your staff and others from harm? | Bespoke surveys – we can tailor a survey to meet your specific needs

- *The Avenue Marketing Centre*
    - Video marketing | Social media marketing | Content marketing | Email marketing | Software tools | Education and training materials

The two linking threads across the three branches are **people** and **communication**. Throughout our work we recognize the significance of the human element of people's working lives and the central role of communication. So, whether, it is a matter of personal and professional development; gauging feedback from groups of staff to improve effectiveness; or getting your important marketing message across, our focus is on helping you achieve the best results at value-for-money prices.

www.avenuemediasolutions.com

Acknowledgements

After 40 years in social work, the number of people I have to thank for helping me develop the knowledge and understanding that have enabled me to produce this manual would make for a very, very long list indeed. So, I will say a general thank you to all those people who have contributed to my learning over the years and reserve my specific thanks for a much smaller group of people.

First must be Dr Sue Thompson, as she has had the single most positive influence on my career and, indeed, on my life. Anna Thompson also deserves thanks for her practical and technical support and for all the other positives having her in my life brings.

My PhD supervisor at Keele University, Colin Richardson, was an enormous source of support and learning. His knowledge, insightfulness and enthusiasm proved invaluable and the positive impact of his place in my life continues to be of major proportions more than a quarter of a century later. This manual is dedicated to his memory.

Clive Curtis, formerly of Cheshire County Council, was for many years an excellent source of learning, as well as a superb role model when it comes to linking theory and practice on a firm foundation of well-developed skills and values. I am delighted to be able to count him among my friends to this day.

The late Jo Campling served as a mentor for much of my publishing career and I owe so much to her for the excellent guidance she gave me, not to mention the friendship and concern.

I have also benefited considerably by having such erudite and supportive friends over the years as Dr John Bates, Dr Jan Pascal, Dr Paul Stepney, Dr Gerry Cox, Dr Dick Gilbert, Dr Darcy Harris, Gerry Skelton, Dr Robert Neimeyer, Dr Kenneth Doka, Dr Inge Corless, Dr Herman de Mönnink, Professor Audrey Mullender, Professor Charlotte Williams, Professor Jason Powell, Professor Bernard Moss and Professor Mark Doel, as well as so many others, not least the La Crosse 'crew' and fellow members of the International Work Group on Death, Dying and Bereavement.

I would also like to thank Professor Mark Doel for his very helpful Foreword and to those valued colleagues who kindly endorsed the value of the manual.

Finally, I would also like to express my gratitude to members of my online learning community, the Avenue Professional Development Programme, for the ongoing stimulation and learning they provide. Thanks, team.

Foreword

Some years back there was a campaign to increase recruitment to social work with a slogan that ran something along the lines of: *Social work. It's all about people. It's as simple and as complex as that.* Though no fan of slogans, I thought this as succinct a statement of social work as you could wish for, and one that managed to convey the paradox of social work practice: a simple desire to change lives alongside an acknowledgement of the complexity of so doing. In a nutshell, it is this paradox that Neil Thompson helps us to grapple with in the pages of this manual.

As you engage with *The Social Worker's Practice Manual*, it will become transparent that social work is a dynamic process of intellectual, emotional and practical activities. It requires analysis, character and strategy in equal measures. Acknowledging which of these is your strongest suit and committing to working harder to improve the others is essential to the development of your social work practice. This manual will put wind in the sails of this voyage of professional self-discovery, one which focuses not just on evidence-based practice but crucially on *practice-based* evidence.

As we have come to expect from the works of Neil Thompson, the human element shines on every page. For example, this means embracing the spirituality of our work with service users; not neglecting self-care; above all, recognizing the people we work with as fellow travellers.

The *context* of social work practice is rightly highlighted. In addition to the broader sociopolitical context, this comprises the local scene – the supervision and employment of the individual practitioner. I gave my heart to social work primarily because of the support of my team leader, John Pettit, in my first job as an unqualified social worker. John understood that each of us has different needs and wants when it comes to defining support and took the trouble to find out what kind of support would sustain and challenge me best. I continue to be reminded of the significance of local context by my eldest daughter, whose emotional temperature as a social worker seems over the years to have correlated with her relationship with her employers and, even more, with her team leaders.

The sections in this manual that consider these contexts – supervisory, organizational, media, structural – are especially telling.

In the pages that follow, you will discover that Neil Thompson employs his ample skill and experience to bring social work practice within fascinating reach and, crucially, to do this without losing the complexities. This is not a 'how to do it' cookbook of practice recipes, nor – heaven forbid – a procedures manual. I see this manual as a 'wise professional', a critical friend who poses questions and dilemmas through a diverse range of practice examples and *moccasin moments* in order to help you think more critically about your own practice and your own practice learning, and to act on that reflection. Social workers who are able to internalize this dialectic process (*'how would my wise professional be prompting me now?'*) are truly able to make a positive difference in the lives of the people they work with. As a profession, social work aims to promote social justice through the accumulation of all these acts of making a difference. *The Social Worker's Practice Manual* will help you to make that difference.

Professor Mark Doel

Preface

By its very nature social work is difficult and challenging work. If situations were simple and straightforward, it is highly unlikely that they would end up on a social worker's desk. Some may see this as a negative, but I view it very positively. That is because the more challenging a situation is, the greater is the potential to make a positive difference. And that, surely, is what it is all about. Also, the more challenging the work is, the greater the opportunity for job satisfaction and a sense of fulfilment.

A key part of social work, then, is managing complexity – being able to look carefully at a situation, appreciate the complexities involved, rather than look for a simple answer (that could make the situation worse) and develop a plan for how best to address the issues involved. This is why I have already mentioned in the *Welcome!* section above that there is such a strong emphasis on reflective practice in our profession.

This reflects the difference between a problem and a puzzle (Thompson, 2012a). A puzzle has a set answer; the task is to work out what *the* answer is. A problem, by contrast, is where there are various potential solutions and the task is to try and work out which is going to be the most appropriate one in the circumstances. This is why, over the years, I have repeatedly said that social work is an intellectual activity; doing it well requires analytical skills, the ability to work with ideas and think things through. This manual, with its emphasis on *practice* is therefore not an alternative to theory and the professional knowledge base. Rather, it is a guide to how to engage with that knowledge base to get the best out of it – what we are aiming for is practice *underpinned* by theory, and certainly not practice as an alternative to theory.

Those analytical skills, and the intelligence they represent, are also needed to achieve the best results within our employing organizations. As I have already mentioned, social work is difficult and challenging by its very nature. However, other factors can sometimes make our role even more difficult and challenging.

Our profession has been facing major difficulties in recent years as a result of wider political and social policy developments that increased family and community pressures, while reducing the investment in, and commitment to, public services ('neoliberalism' is the technical term for this). There is therefore a significant clash between what social workers are trying to do at the grass roots and what is happening at a macro level. The important connection between these two levels is generally the organizations that employ social workers.

 How effective such organizations are in supporting their staff through such difficulties varies enormously. Some social workers are fortunate to work in supportive teams, with supportive managers. Others are not so fortunate. In my view, the quality of employer support can be crucial, which is one of the main reasons why one of my main interests is in leadership (Thompson, 2013; 2016b). But, it is also important to note that we can influence, to a certain extent, the organizations we work for. These challenges are also part of what we need to prepare for, and so elements of 'workplace survival' are to be found in this manual too.

I very much hope that you will find this manual a useful resource to help you to be the best social worker you can be. The people we serve deserve that, and so do you.

Introduction

The manual is divided into 30 sections. I refer to them as sections, rather than chapters, to emphasize that this is a practice-focused manual, an active resource for you to *use*, rather than a conventional textbook for you to refer to. Each section covers what I regard as one of the core elements of good practice in social work. Although 30 may seem a lot, it is still not exhaustive – there are far more than 30 aspects to social work. However, what you will find here should give you a firm foundation on which to build.

Each section highlights some key issues and ends with a space for you to note down your own ideas, a place for your own reflections. Please don't skip past these. This is not a textbook where you can pick and choose what ideas you do or do not focus on. Everything covered is important for good practice, and so it is essential that you think the issues through to form your own view, as that is what is going to be guiding your practice. In other words, what is important is not what *I* teach, but what *you* learn – your own response to the issues is what counts. To put it quite frankly, if you are not thinking about the issues and forming your own view, then you are wasting your time, as reading what I think without 'processing' that to make your own sense of it will do you no good whatsoever.

It may be that one or more sections will not be directly relevant to you. For example, the section on court work may have no bearing on your work if, in your setting, court work is not a feature. However, where a section is of relevance to you (and that will be the vast majority of them), then please do make sure that you get the learning benefits from what is on offer.

Why a manual?

The word 'manual' comes from the Latin word for hand (as in manual labour, manual dexterity and so on), so a manual is a *hand*book. By 'handbook' what I mean is a set of guidelines that can help in direct practice. It is not the sort of text you might scan through to look for a quote to include in an essay; it is a basis for practice. For students, this means that it is likely to be of more use to you on placement (or in preparing for placement) than in your academic work. For practising social workers, it is likely to be of more use to you in reviewing and consolidating your practice than in pursuing any further or higher qualifications. It is about *making a difference*.

But don't confuse the idea of a handbook, in the sense that I am using it here, with a 'procedures manual' or set of instructions. As I have already emphasized, social work is far too complex to simply follow instructions. Each section provides food for thought and insights from my own extensive experience plus what I have learned from being a social work manager, consultant, expert witness and educator. I estimate that I have run something in the region of 2,000 training courses over the years, so that is an awful lot of conversations that I have been able to learn from, an awful lot of unofficial, informal research that has taught me what people struggle with, how things go wrong and, just as importantly, what works well. This manual is therefore a distillation of that learning.

Imagine the manual as a senior colleague whose experience and knowledge you can draw on to help and guide you, but not simply as someone who will tell you what to do or make your decisions for you.

Who is it for?

I envisage five groups of people potentially finding this manual useful:

- Students on placement or preparing to go out on placement;
- Newly qualified social workers wanting guidance and reassurance as they make the adjustment from student to fully fledged social worker;
- Experienced social workers who want to make sure that they are keeping 'in touch' with practice issues and are not just slotting into habits and set procedures – in other words, it can be a resource to aid reflective practice;
- Managers who wish to make sure that they are well placed to offer guidance and support to the staff they supervise and lead;
- Educators, whether in academic settings or in practice agencies, who wish to use the insights offered here to help the learners they are supporting.

Of course, different groups may use the manual in different ways, but, whichever group you are in, you should be able to make this work for you.

How do I use it?

To get the best out of this manual, I would suggest that you read it through from start to finish fairly quickly to begin with. Then, once you have got a sense of what it is all about, you can come back and study each section more closely, making a note of your own views and issues. It would make sense to do this in the order in which the sections are presented within the manual. However, if there is any reason why you would want to bring forward studying a particular area, then there is nothing to stop you from doing so, provided that you don't forget to go back at some point to any sections you missed out in doing so.

But, please do remember my earlier plea. This is not a textbook just to be read, it is a manual to be *used*, a resource to aid you with your thinking and in developing your own approach. So, please do make sure you give the issues some thought and keep a record of your reflections – otherwise you are just going through the motions, and that won't really help anyone.

1. Begin at the beginning

If we are going to focus on *practising* social work, perhaps we need to be clear about what it is, who needs it and what good it can do – and that is precisely what we are going to focus on in this first section.

What is social work?

The question is only four words in length, but it is still a very big question! There are very big debates to be had about the nature of social work (see the discussion in my *Understanding Social Work* book – Thompson, 2015a), but what I want to emphasize here is that we need to be very clear about the boundaries of our work, the boundaries of social work.

So, rather than present you with a simple answer to the question, I am going to set you a challenge, namely:

> *At all times you need to be clear: Is what I am being asked to do (or what I feel I should do) appropriate within my social work role?*

As I see it, social work is a process of being a creative helper, but not just providing any help in any circumstances. The boundaries of our roles as creative helpers are determined in large part by relevant legislation, social policies, organizational policies, our professional values and the pragmatic requirements of each specific situation we engage in.

 It is very easy to be drawn here and there by different pressures and demands, but we must keep a clear focus on our social work role at all times.

Being clear about what our role should be is not always easy. It is a key part of *assessment*, a crucial aspect of social work practice that we will keep coming back to throughout this manual.

How social work will be carried out will, of course, vary from setting to setting, context to context, but, whatever form it takes, we will need to keep a clear focus on its core elements, not least the professional knowledge, skills and values that we will be discussing later.

This diversity should not be confused with vagueness. Many times I have had to challenge people who say that 'social work is so vague, isn't it?'. My response has consistently been: 'It is only vague if done vaguely' (see the discussion of systematic practice in Section 23). Consider, for  example, how the forms nursing takes might differ greatly across, say, an accident and emergency unit, a genito-urinary ward, a geriatric ward or a well-woman clinic, but it would still be seen as underpinned by core nursing principles – it would be seen as diverse, rather than vague. Social work is equally diverse and also has its core foundations – anyone who sees social work as 'vague' is therefore unaware of those foundations or has lost sight of them (see Thompson, 2016c).

Who needs social work?

Many years ago a writer by the name of Hugh England made a comment that has stuck with me over the years. In a nutshell, he argued that everyone has problems; we all have challenges and difficulties that we need to deal with. However, some people have problems in dealing with their problems, difficulties in managing their difficulties (England, 1986).

What this means is that some people's life challenges are more challenging than is the case for most others. This can be for various reasons, not least: poverty and deprivation; discrimination and oppression; disability; infirmity or vulnerability related to age and/or health concerns; alcohol or other drug dependency; loss, grief and trauma; stress; mental health problems; and various other social and personal factors.

We also have to take time into consideration. What I mean by this is that some people may need social work at particular times, but not at others. For example, parents who experience a particular set of difficulties may, for a while, have difficulties in meeting their children's needs, resulting in concerns about neglect, but, with appropriate support to get them through that difficult patch, they may then be perfectly capable of meeting their children's needs thereafter. Similarly an elderly couple experiencing various difficulties may be able to just about cope in the community while they are together, but, when one partner is admitted to hospital after a fall, the other may not be able to cope alone. Social work support may therefore be needed for a short period, but not thereafter.

This emphasis on time helps to prevent dependency creation. It is important that we do not label people as being in need of social work support as if it is some sort of character flaw or personal weakness. Our assessment needs to be much more sophisticated than that, as we shall see.

*** KEY POINT ***

Assessment is the process of gathering information, forming a picture of the situation and developing a plan for how we respond to it. It is the core foundation of good practice.

So, the question of who needs social work is a complex one to answer, reflecting the complex nature of social work itself.

One aspect of this that it is important for us to bear in mind is that demand is infinite, but supply is finite. What I mean by this is that any number of people could need our help at any given time, but there is, of course, a limit to how many people we can help or how much we can help each person who comes our way. We therefore have to: (i) have a clear sense of priorities, being clear as far as possible whose need for our help is greatest; (ii) not waste time or resources; (iii) be able to redirect people to other sources of help as appropriate ('signposting'), rather than duplicating efforts by doing things that others are able to do; and (iv) focus on empowerment rather than dependency creation – that is, helping people to address their own problems as far as possible by exploring creative solutions (rather than simply thinking in terms of providing services – see the discussion of consumerism in Section 23).

Unfortunately, some people oversimplify this complex matter of balancing finite resources against potentially infinite demand by reducing it to a simple matter of saving money. The net result is that much-needed help is not provided or not provided soon enough, leading to a situation where the problem gets worse and ends up eating up even more resources. There is a complex and difficult balancing act to be managed here to

make sure that: (i) scarce resources are not wasted (for example, when other solutions could have been brought to bear or where a service continues to be provided when it is no longer needed, having not been reviewed properly); and (ii) we make the best possible use of the resources available to us (including social work time, of course) – resourcefulness is one of the essential three Rs that we will discuss in Section 3. This is one of the reasons why, throughout my teaching and training work I have emphasized the importance of time and workload management. There are important skills to be learned in this regard, although it is sadly the case that many social workers seem to try to manage a heavy workload without exploring – let alone learning – those essential skills (see Thompson, 2015b).

We need an intelligent, reflective approach to these issues, one that both reflects and addresses the complexity involved. It comes back to the idea that, in effect, doing social work involves managing complexity.

What is the value of social work?

Another big question! But it is an important one. There is an interesting (and unfortunate) discrepancy between media representations of social work as problematic and of limited value and the actual reality of high levels of satisfaction with social support that have consistently been revealed from 'consumer' research relating to social services provision.

An important lesson from this is that we should not be discouraged by negative press; we should not allow the biased reporting of certain publications that make money from telling sensationalized stories that feed popular prejudices and stereotypes to distract our attention from the fact that what we do is important and worthwhile and makes a huge positive difference (for the most part) to the people we serve. See Jones (2014) for an important discussion of the distorting role of the media.

So, what is the value of social work, then? The following benefits are just some of the ways in which social work can have immense value:

➢ *Preventing family breakdown* Various forms of family support can help to keep families together and prevent the significant distress associated with family breakdown.

➢ *Keeping people in the community* Community care support measures can play a key role in preventing the need for vulnerable people to enter institutions. Promoting independence is therefore an important part of the story of what value social work can offer.

➢ *Preventing abuse* There is no guaranteed way of preventing abuse, of course, but social work interventions when suspicions are raised or abuse indicators become apparent have prevented abuse in a large number of cases and will continue to do so.

➢ *Responding to abuse* Once abuse issues arise, whether child abuse or the abuse of vulnerable adults, there is much that social workers can do to support the people so affected, not least in preventing further abuse.

➢ *Dealing with the aftermath of abuse* A common consequence of abuse is trauma, and social work support can be invaluable in helping people recover from trauma and its detrimental consequences.

➢ *Providing alternative care* Whether for children or adults, there is often an important role for social workers in providing alternative care or accommodation when circumstances arise that mean that pre-existing arrangements are no longer adequate.

➢ *Corporate parenting* For many children leaving their family home is necessary for their needs to be met. In such circumstances there is an important role for social workers to act *in loco parentis* – that is, to do as much as reasonably possible to ensure that the children concerned are well parented.

➢ *Aiding recovery* Whether in relation to physical or mental health problems, social work can play an invaluable role in helping people to recover from the challenges they have been experiencing.

➢ *Improving quality of life* Helping people with disabilities to be more independent would be one example of the various ways in which social work can be of value in promoting well-being.

➢ *Preparing young people for independence* Children who have spent much of their childhood in foster or residential care will need considerable support in making the transition to independent living. High-quality social work can make a very positive difference in this regard.

➤ *Public protection* This can be in relation to abuse issues, crime and anti-social behaviour, drug-related problems or other such issues that can pose a threat to citizens.

It should be clear, then, that social work is a very valuable undertaking when done properly. Making sure that it is indeed done properly is a major part of what this manual is all about.

 Social work is a positive power for good that makes a hugely positive difference. Never let the negativity surrounding social work lead you to lose sight of how important and worthwhile social work is.

2. Attitudes and values

Attitudes and values can make a huge difference in social work, positively or negatively. So, in this section, we consider some important issues relating to how attitudes and values need to be understood and their significance appreciated.

Why are you in social work?

Different people come into social work for different reasons. But, whatever the reasons, it is important that you are clear about what they are and not lose sight of them. Why? Because, as I have already indicated, social work is by its very nature a demanding occupation, but to that we also need to add the challenges of working in underfunded organizations and within a sociopolitical context of neoliberalism in which public services in general and social work in particular are not valued. So, we need to recognize that social work is characterized by struggle, and, at times, that struggle can be of significant proportions. At such times, we need to be clear about why we came into social work and – crucially – the values that informed that decision. Our values are a key part of what motivates and sustains us. We lose sight of them at our peril.

Values are, by definition, what we value, what we hold dear – they are the beliefs and principles that matter to us. Much of the time they are submerged and invisible, but they are still there. They will influence us in a number of ways, not least in relation to our thoughts, feelings and actions (see the discussion of the Think-Feel-Do framework in my *People Skills* book – Thompson, 2015b).

➤ *Thoughts* What we think and how we think will be shaped in part by our values. For example, if dignity is part of our value base, then in carrying out an assessment and developing a plan, it is likely that we will seek to ensure that what we produce will in no way infringe anyone's dignity. By contrast, if dignity were not part of our value base, we may well be developing plans that pay no heed to people's dignity.

➤ *Feelings* Our feelings and emotional reactions also have much to do with values. For example, if equality and social justice are part of your value base, you are likely to experience anger when encountering a situation in which one or more people are being treated unfairly or are being discriminated against. Values therefore play a key role where emotion is concerned. Consequently, there is practical value in considering not only our own emotional responses, but also those of others. If you are puzzled by someone's emotional reaction to a situation, consider their values and how they are influencing the situation.

➤ *Actions* The fact that you are in social work is, in all likelihood, a reflection of your values. As I have already mentioned, social work is a difficult and demanding job, so what is it about your set of values that makes you willing to expose yourself to such difficulties and risks? There are much easier ways of making a living, but these would not be as rewarding or enriching as social work, so what does that tell you about your value base?

Values are complex and tricky entities and are generally not things that we can see or detect directly. To work out where and how values are operating, we need to look at their effects. For example, we may not be able to witness 'compassion' as a raw value in its abstract state, but we can certainly recognize examples of compassion when we see them. Values therefore reveal themselves through their consequences.

There is a parallel here with love. We cannot see love in its raw, abstract state, but we have no difficulty recognizing its effects; we easily notice acts of love.

Over the years many people have told me they feel uncomfortable with the idea of values, because they are so abstract. They feel happier, so they have told me, with more concrete entities. However, this type of thinking fails to recognize just how concrete values are – just how much of a concrete impact they have on us and on the people we serve and support. That impact can be incredibly positive and constructive or enormously negative and destructive – hence the need to be very tuned in to the significance of values. People who profess no interest in values because they are 'abstract' are not only missing the point, but also following a highly risky and potentially harmful strategy.

So, there are two key points to emphasize: (i) values are extremely important and we neglect them at our peril; and (ii) our values are a key part of why we are in social work.

 It is essential that we do not lose sight of our values, as they are a key part of why we are in social work. They are also highly significant in relation to thoughts, feelings and actions. We need to keep coming back to our values time and time again.

Why are you in this person's life?

There is a fine but highly significant line between *intervention* (the technical terms for what we do in helping people) and *interference* (being an unwelcome and inappropriate presence in someone's life). The former is ethical, the latter is certainly not. This means that, at all times, we need to be clear why we are in someone's life and whether it can be justified.

One of the main reasons for this is that, in practising social work, we are exercising power, and so we have to make sure that we are using that power wisely and appropriately – that is, ethically. There is a danger here that, because we can often *feel* relatively powerless, we can easily forget that we *are* powerful. At times it may seem that it is managers, panels that manage budgets, courts or others who hold the power, and we have none. But, this is dangerously misleading, of course, as there are various ways in which, as social workers, we exercise power. Losing sight of this can lead to oppressive practices.

There are certain circumstances where we can justify being involved in someone's life against their will or without their consent (for example, protecting children from abuse or working with someone whose mental health problems make them a danger to themselves or other people). However, the fact that there are certain limited and specific circumstances where this is permitted does not mean that we are not constrained in all other circumstances from being involved without consent.

In those specific situations where our involvement is without the full consent of the people concerned, it is especially important that we are clear about why we are there, but this clarity is important in *all* cases. We have no right whatsoever to be in people's lives without good reason.

>>> Moccasins moment <<<

How would you feel if a social worker were visiting your family, but you were not clear why or for what purpose? What attitude would you have towards that social worker and perhaps social workers in general as a result of that?

This fits with the idea of systematic practice to be discussed in Section 23 where the importance of having clarity about the outcomes we are trying to achieve is emphasized. As we shall see when get to Section 23, it is very easy for various pressures and distractions to lead us to lose sight of what we are trying to achieve and therefore why, in effect, we are in this person's life.

Personal and professional values

One of the strong expectations in social work is that you will be committed to the professional values associated with it. Imagine if practitioners had no commitment to confidentiality as a professional value and people's private information was being passed about with no concern for their privacy. Clearly, then, professional values are not an optional extra.

However, having said that, I have come across a few people who have argued that values are a personal matter and employers should have no right to seek to impose any values on them. I can see where they are coming from when they say this, as values are quite personal in a sense – indeed, to a large extent, they are part of who we are. Our sense of self will often revolve around certain value commitments. However, to say that employers are seeking to 'impose' values and should not be doing so is an oversimplification of some complex issues.

No one is forced to become a social worker; it is a free choice. In making that choice we are also making a commitment to the profession's values – that is, in a sense, a condition of joining the profession. Anyone who were to say, for example: 'I have no interest in dignity and I am strongly in favour of discriminating against minority groups' would not be accepted into the profession in the first place. So, there is no 'imposing' of values – a commitment to certain values is a requirement for the job, just as a commitment to helping children learn would be a requirement of being a teacher or being committed to helping people get better would be a requirement of being a nurse. Again, there is no 'imposing' going on.

Imagine a parallel example: Sam applies for a job as a sales assistant. At the interview it is made clear that a commitment to the value of customer service is a requirement of the job. Sam's response is that values are a personal matter and employers have no right to impose them. Quite right, says the interviewer, you are entitled to your values, but we are entitled not to employ anyone who is not committed to customer care.

As we noted earlier, values are not 'abstract' and unimportant in concrete, real-life situations; they are highly significant and influential. Anyone whose values do not fit with what the profession (whether sales or social work) requires would be more of a liability than an asset.

Making a commitment to professional values is not generally a negation of your own personal values. Indeed, in my experience, the vast majority of social workers have a *personal* value commitment to treating people with respect, promoting equality and fairness and so on. Consequently, their personal and professional values reinforce and strengthen one another. However, there can be times occasionally when personal and professional values clash. For example, a social worker who has strong Catholic beliefs may have difficulty working with a teenage girl who has become pregnant as a result of abuse and is now seeking to have an abortion. Of course, such situations need sensitive handling, but, in my experience, can usually be managed effectively without any great problems. We should not allow these rare exceptions to distract us from the fact that personal and professional value are usually quite compatible.

*** KEY POINT ***

Values are a basic element of the foundations of social work. They are subtle and complex matters, and so we need to keep learning about them. We should never lose sight of them or take them for granted.

Values Exercise

In Chapter 5 of my *Understanding Social Work* book I list some core social work values as:

Confidentiality | Respect for persons | Social justice | Partnership

Consider each of these in turn to make sure you are clear what they mean and how they apply to you and your work.

3. Being prepared

What can we do to make sure that we are as well equipped as possible to rise to the challenges that are involved in social work? One important part of the answer to that question is that we can *be prepared*. And that is precisely what Section 3 is all about. Daniel Pink, in his important book about motivation (Pink, 2011), draws a distinction between types of work that are *algorithmic* (that is, the follow set patterns and routines) and those that are *heuristic* (that is, they need to be thought through, as there is no set course of action to follow). I made the point earlier that social work is not 'painting by numbers' – it requires skill, artistry, creative thinking and resourcefulness. It is not simply a matter of walking into a situation and following a set path – the reality of social work is far more complex than that, of course. We can never be entirely sure what we are walking into, and that is why we need to be prepared.

We are going to look at the subject of 'being prepared' under three headings: social work knowledge; the three Rs and the importance of confidence.

Social work knowledge

'It's not fair', a social work assistant once said to me, 'social workers get paid a lot more than I do, just because they have a piece of paper'. I tried to convince her that it was not the piece of paper itself that mattered, but the extensive knowledge base it represents – a knowledge base that is essential to being an effective social worker. But she was not convinced. 'Social work is just common sense', she added.

Understandable though this perception may be, it is not only inaccurate, but dangerously so. Consider the following examples of the central role of professional knowledge in helping us appreciate the complexities of what we are dealing with.

- A child is functioning at a developmental level well below what would be expected of someone of their age. A social worker who is not familiar with at least a basic understanding of child development could miss the significance of this. This could be highly problematic if this developmental delay were being caused by abuse.

- A man is highly anxious, while also showing signs of depression. It is important that the social worker has a good understanding of these issues in order to form a positive and empathic working relationship with him. A lack of awareness of the significance of anxiety and depression could leave the social worker ill-equipped for their role and leave the man feeling mistrustful of the worker (potentially making the anxiety and depression worse).

- An older woman has become withdrawn and isolated; she seems to have lost all interest in life and is neglecting herself. In this way she is placing herself at considerable risk of harm. A social worker who understands both the impact of cumulative grief (loss after loss after loss) and the insidiously undermining effects of ageism will be much better equipped to help than someone who thinks it is all a matter of common sense and sets about on a simplistic process of trying to cheer her up and encourage her to have more social contacts.

- Faced with a family with multiple complex problems there can be a tendency to be judgemental and simply see them as a 'problem family' or as dysfunctional, as if the problems are simply down to the personal inadequacies of the individual family members. This is highly unlikely to help and could, in fact, cause significant problems. A more sophisticated understanding would include an appreciation of family dynamics, power relations, poverty and social stigma and so on.

I could go on giving example after example, but I do not want to labour the point. Our professional knowledge will not give us everything we need by way of understanding of the complexities involved, but it will give us a helpful foundation on which to build over time as we learn and develop and draw out the lessons from our growing experience.

Our knowledge base should give us at least some understanding of, amongst other things:

- The wider social context and how it affects people's lives, their problems and the potential solutions. Without this understanding we run the risk of focusing too narrowly on individual factors and losing sight of the big picture.

 • Interpersonal dynamics – each interaction involving two or more people will be unique in its own right, but there will also be patterns discernible. For example, there will be significant patterns of language use, nonverbal communication and established social rules, roles, rites and rituals.

- Problems, their nature, significance, impact and potential solutions. This will include social problems, family problems and personal problems – the various life challenges we face.

- Tools and methods for addressing problems, meeting needs and promoting empowerment.

- Discrimination and oppression and the various ways in which these have a detrimental effect on people's lives (and how we can make things worse) if we are not tuned in to the issues involved.

- Risk assessment and management – an oversimplified or ill-informed approach to these issues can cause considerable problems for ourselves and the people we are seeking to help.

These are just some of the areas of knowledge that are relevant to social work – the full list could easily take up a whole book and still be far from comprehensive.

It is also important to recognize that our knowledge base is useful – and necessary – not only for the *understanding* we need to tackle the challenges we face, but also to develop the skills we need. For example, our understanding of interpersonal interactions (drawing on psychological and sociological insights) can be a sound foundation for developing our communication skills. Of course, we learn basic communication skills as part of our upbringing, but in a job like social work, we need to be able to take our communications skills to a more advanced level than just everyday interactions. Our everyday skills may not be enough to help us respond effectively to someone who is distressed, depressed, defensive, anxious, aggressive or alarmed. They will also leave us ill-equipped to manage conflict beyond a very basic level. As we develop our knowledge base we are then in a position to develop the associated skills and take them to a more advanced level.

And, of course, both the knowledge and the skills need to be underpinned by values, as we noted in Section 2. Without values the power offered by such knowledge and skills could be misused and do harm. This 'triad' of knowledge, skills and values is an important one to bear in mind.

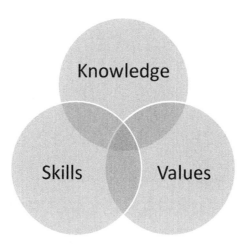

Being well prepared therefore rests, in part, on being well informed. Being well informed, in turn, means continuing to learn. Sadly, the important term 'continuous professional development' (or CPD for short) has to a large extent been reduced in some quarters simply to ticking boxes to prevent potential problems with professional (re-)registration. In reality, though, continuous professional development is about the need to keep learning, to continue to grow and develop in order to make sure that we are able to produce the best results possible (so that we can have the most positive impact and enjoy the fullest rewards for our efforts). We shall return to this point in Sections 8 and 30.

 The problems and challenges we encounter in social work are often complex and highly demanding. Trying to tackle them in an uninformed way is highly risky for all concerned. We should therefore make full use of the knowledge base available to us.

The three Rs

In an earlier work I discussed the importance of what I called the three Rs: resourcefulness, robustness and resilience. These are also important elements of what we need in order to be as reasonably prepared as we can to cope with social work practice and its heavy demands. So, what I am going to do here is to revisit these three Rs and highlight how an understanding of them can be helpful by giving us a useful framework that we can apply to ourselves and to the people we serve. We shall look at each of these in turn, highlighting the practice implications involved.

Resourcefulness

By resourcefulness what I mean is the ability to be creative and imaginative, to be innovative in helping people find solutions to their problems, ways to meet their needs and taking steps towards empowerment. The challenges we face come in a myriad of shapes and sizes, different colours and shades and different textures. A simple formula response is likely to be woefully inadequate. The more resourceful we can be in helping people to face their challenges, the better equipped we will be to meet our own. This involves:

- Having access to a wider range of potential solutions or positive ways forward;
- Not being restricted to formulaic responses;
- Seeing aspects of the situation you might not have otherwise noticed;

- Creating opportunities for learning – for yourself and for other people involved; and
- Generating hope – something that can make a huge positive difference in some circumstances.

Resourcefulness can be seen as important for practice in at least three ways:

1. *Developing your own resourcefulness* There is much to be gained from developing our own resourcefulness. It is not a 'quality' you either have or do not have. It is a set of skills and, as such, those skills can be learned, developed and improved upon (see, for example, Chapter 8 of my *People Skills* book).

2. *Recognizing resourcefulness in others* When people come to us for help they are often at a low ebb and struggling. At such times the negatives of a situation can be very much to the fore. Consequently, there can be a danger that the strengths and positives involved will be missed  (Desai, 2018). This includes people's resourcefulness. When we see the difficulties they are currently having, we may find it difficult to appreciate their resourcefulness – for example, in terms of how well they have coped to date. Many of the individuals and families we deal with demonstrate high levels of resourcefulness and such examples are not hard to find. It would therefore be a significant mistake to fail to account for their resourcefulness and, indeed, to capitalize on it as fully as possible.

3. *Developing resourcefulness in others* While many of the people we are supporting may well demonstrate high levels of resourcefulness, we need to be aware that not all will. Some people may be struggling partly because they have adopted a restricted, limited or rigid approach to the challenges they face. In such circumstances one of the ways in which we could be helpful is not only to bring our own resourcefulness to bear, but also to help them develop their own resourcefulness. This could be seen as part of

the educational approach to social work (Thompson, 2016c) and also a significant contribution to empowerment - helping people to gain greater control over their lives.

Resourcefulness, then, is clearly an important concept to bear in mind in developing effective forms of practice. It is not, though, the only one. It dovetails well with robustness and so it is to that that we now turn.

>>> Moccasins moment <<<

Imagine that you or your family needed help from a social worker and the approach that worker adopted was to simply follow a set pattern, to stay within narrow tramlines – showing no signs of resourcefulness. Imagine, too, that they took no account of your resourcefulness or made no attempt to develop it. Would you be happy with that approach? Would you see that as acceptable practice?

Robustness

Being robust means being able to withstand pressure. It does not mean being tough, macho or unfeeling. Being able to withstand pressure depends on a number of factors, not least the following:

➢ *The type of pressure* Each of us is different in terms of how much pressure we are able to handle, depending in large part on our life experiences to date and the lessons we have learned – or not learned – from that experience. However, we are also different in terms of the *types* of pressure we can handle. For example, some people are better at managing tension than others. Consider how some people can do public speaking tasks and just take it all in their stride, while others really struggle to cope with the tension. Likewise, some people are very skilled at handling emotional challenges, while others find them much more difficult.

➤ *The intensity of the pressure* How intense or severe the pressure is will also be very relevant. Everyone has their breaking point, of course, and once again this will largely depend on our experience and learning around these issues. There is a subjective element to this too, in the sense that much depends on how we *perceive* the pressure (again reflecting our experience and learning). For example, someone who has been on the receiving end of significant violence may be highly sensitized to the risk of violence and thus experience another person's aggressive attitude as more of a threat (and thus a more intense pressure) than would be the case for someone who has never encountered a serious level of violence.

➤ *The number of pressures* Sometimes there will be pressures that are manageable on their own, but become too much when they arise in combination. Indeed, the point where the last straw is reached may well be the point at which referral to a social worker is made. When I was a student social worker I was taught to ask people making referrals: Why now? Why contact us at this point? This was because problems had usually been going on for quite a while before a referral was eventually made. So, very often what would emerge from asking that question was a comment to the effect that the situation had now got worse, but what also became apparent quite often was that another pressure had arisen. For example, the older person struggling to cope alone in the community was not referred to a social worker until they became ill and thus had another set of pressures to contend with – they could just about cope unaided when in good health, but even a minor illness was enough to make the situation unmanageable as it stood.

➤ *The timespan* How long the pressure goes on for will also be significant. Again, we all have our limits, and so while we may be able to cope with certain pressures for a certain amount of time, we can reach a point where we can stand it no more, we have reached the end of our tether.

➤ *The level and quality of support* All the above points are important, but this one particularly so. It is very easy to be judgemental about robustness – for example, by dismissing certain people as weak, flaky or even inadequate. How effectively people cope will depend on: (i) lessons learned from previous experiences; and (ii) the level and quality of support. The latter can be a key factor in empowering us to handle the pressure we face, whereas its absence can add to the pressures and undermine our confidence in our ability to cope (Thompson, 2015c). Support can also be instrumental in helping us draw out the lessons from our previous pressure experiences. Support is therefore crucial. This has two key practice implications for us: (i) we should not hesitate to seek and use support to help us with our own pressures (again, we should not equate robustness with being macho); and (ii) we should appreciate the key role we can play as social workers in helping people to manage their pressures effectively.

So, how do we develop our own robustness and help others to develop theirs? Well, there is no simple or straightforward answer to that. Much will depend on the circumstances and also on how skilled and experienced we are in using the various social work tools and methods available to us (Thompson, 2012a; Thompson and Stepney, 2018). And, of course, much of that will depend on our resourcefulness, of course!

As we are about to see, both resourcefulness and robustness also need to be understood in the context of resilience, the third of our three Rs.

Resilience

This is a topic that has been receiving increasing attention in social work and the other caring professions. It is often referred to as 'bouncebackability'. Robustness refers to our ability to withstand pressure and thus avoid adversity; resilience refers to our ability to get back on our feet after experiencing adversity. So, when the pressures reach the point that they knock us down, resilience is what gets us back up again and gets us back into coping mode.

As with resourcefulness, there are three elements to this:

- *Recognizing our own resilience* – developing it and capitalizing on it wherever possible.

- *Recognizing other people's resilience* – again, we should not underestimate how resilient people can already be, how many times they have picked themselves up and carried on.

- *Developing other people's resilience* – there are various ways in which we can contribute to empowerment by helping people develop their resilience. As with robustness, support is again a central feature of this.

There are no set ways of achieving greater resilience, our own or other people's, but there is much that – with a resourceful, well-informed approach – we can do to move in a positive direction.

If you think carefully about the 3Rs it should not be too difficult for you to realize that they are interlinked and support one another. Being resourceful will make it easier for us to be robust and resilient. Being robust will give us greater confidence to be resourceful and will help us to be resilient. Being resilient will give us opportunities to learn and thus to be more resourceful. Bouncing back from adversity in this way will also help us to be more robust.

It is therefore helpful to think of the three Rs as a framework of understanding that can be a useful tool in practice, rather than simply three sets of issues that just happen to start with the letter R. Bearing this framework in mind can be a very useful preparation for practice.

Resourcefulness

Robustness

Resilience

Finally, in terms of the three Rs, it is important to stress that each one is not a quality that you either have or do not have. Each of them is a set of skills that can be *learned*. And, given the way the three elements are intertwined, developing our skills in one can help us to develop our skills in the other two.

Confidence

The third element of being prepared that we are going to look at is that of confidence. Literally, confidence means trust. 'I have confidence in you' means 'I trust you'. Similarly, confidential information is sensitive information that you are being trusted with.

It can be helpful to recognize that there are two main types of confidence, subjective and objective. Subjective confidence is self-confidence; it reflects the level of self-confidence you have, the extent to which you trust yourself. So, being confident that you can achieve a particular task amounts to trusting yourself to be able to complete that task.

Objective confidence is the trust *other people* have in you. How much faith they have in you to be reliable and so on will be what objective confidence is all about. It reflects your *credibility*. This is very important because, in social work, much of what we do involves trying to influence people in a positive direction (see Section 6). It is difficult if not impossible to influence people if you have little or no credibility. Objective confidence is therefore very important indeed – we will struggle considerably without it.

However, what is also important to recognize is that subjective and objective confidence are interlinked – they have a significant impact on each other. For example, if I were to have no confidence in myself, it is likely that people will notice this (through my nonverbal communication, for example), and the likely consequence of this is that they will have little faith in me (a lack of subjective confidence can lead to a lack of objective confidence). Likewise, if I were to have a supervisor who had no faith in me (through no fault of my own, as a form of bullying perhaps), that may well reduce my self-confidence (a lack of objective confidence is likely to reduce subjective confidence). The same can happen in positive terms too – that is increasing one form of confidence is likely to increase the other.

The implications of this are twofold:

1. Failing to have self-belief is likely to come at a high cost. Without subjective confidence we will struggle to achieve objective confidence (credibility and trust) and will therefore be very poorly placed when it comes to seeking to influence people in a positive direction (which is, of course, a key part of what we do in social work). We cannot afford not to have confidence in ourselves; we have to start from a position of self-belief.

2. If we become aware of any factors that are standing in the way of having a high level of objective confidence, we need to do something about it. For example, if someone is operating from a stereotypical basis of understanding and is therefore prejudiced against social workers, it would be unwise to try to ignore this. Challenging it constructively would be a much wiser course of action. We cannot afford not to have credibility and therefore need to do whatever we reasonably can to boost our objective confidence (and that, in turn, should help to boost our subjective confidence).

Preparing yourself

A great deal could have been covered under the heading of 'Being prepared', certainly far more than we have space for here. However, what we have focused on here should be sufficient to give you a clear picture of some of the key issues involved. In a nutshell, to be prepared for high-quality social work, you will need knowledge (to make sure that you are well informed and have a good level of understanding), skills (to enable you to use that knowledge in effective ways in practice), values (to make sure your actions are safe and ethical) and confidence (to show that you have faith in yourself and to promote others having faith in you).

Confidence Exercise

What steps can you take to ensure that your confidence – subjective and objective – is a strength that you can rely on, rather than a weakness that can let you (and the people you serve) down? Who is best placed to help you with this?

4. Making a difference

In a sense, making a difference is precisely what social work is all about. What would be the point of engaging in social work activities if we ended up making no difference? So, what is involved in 'making a difference' in a social work sense? That is precisely what we are going to look at now. We shall look at the important idea of 'theorizing practice', examine the part played by social work processes, revisit the importance of social work skills and also explore the range of tools available to us that can assist us in making that difference.

Theorizing practice

The traditional approach to the relationship between theory and practice can be characterized by the idea that we should 'apply theory to practice' – that is, begin with theory, our professional knowledge base, and then try to 'apply' it to practice. However, in my work, I have argued that it makes much more sense to begin with practice, real-life situations, and then explore how our knowledge base can cast light on the circumstances we find ourselves in (Thompson, 2017a). This is what I mean by 'theorizing' practice. We begin with practice and then *theorize* it by drawing on our knowledge base to make sense of it.

This fits well with the idea of reflective practice (see Section 10) which requires us to approach our work thoughtfully, intelligently and in a way that is informed by our professional knowledge base (as well as our professional skills and values). Consider the following examples:

➢ A referral is received relating to an 86-year-old woman who is living alone in the community and is struggling to cope. A request is made that she should be admitted to residential care 'for her own good' This immediately raises a number of questions:

- Does this person want help or is she quite happy as she is? Is involvement in her life justified by the level of concern of the referrer?
- What exactly is meant by 'struggling to cope'? In what way? To what extent? What risks are involved? What counterbalances are there to the risks?
- If the risks are at an unacceptable level, would residential care be necessary or could a package of community care support services be sufficient to address the concerns? Does the woman concerned share the view of the level of risk involved or is she under pressure from others who would feel happier if she were in residential care? What are her rights? What is your role in safeguarding her rights?
- To what extent might ageism be a factor – for example, a reliance on ageist stereotypes of older people being dependent and in need of looking after?

These are just some of the many questions that could arise. They may, at first glance, seem fairly basic, but each one of them could easily be glossed over by someone who does not have a social work knowledge base to draw upon.

➢ A social worker has been supervising a 14-year-old girl who is in foster care. A teacher rings the social worker to say that the girl has told the school nurse that she has been sexually abused by her foster father. This too raises a number of important questions:

- How do we make sure that the girl concerned is safe? What risks are involved? How do we balance them?
- What actions are required under the relevant safeguarding procedures?
- Who needs to be involved? In what capacity?
- What constitutes abuse? How serious does it need to be?
- What harm can abuse do? Has the girl been traumatized?
- If the alleged abuse is confirmed, what needs to happen?

The questions could go on, each one potentially leading to other questions. Clearly, these are complex issues that need to be handled sensitively. Without a well-developed knowledge base of the key issues involved, we could be making a bad situation worse or at least failing to make a positive difference.

> Tim spent several months in an in-patient psychiatric unit following the death of his wife and son in a road traffic accident. On discharge he had made good progress and was able to cope reasonably well with his life and its challenges. Now, however, he has started to deteriorate quite rapidly and his GP felt that a further admission may be needed, on a compulsory basis if needed. Of course, this scenario raises several questions too:

   o What 'triggers' may be operating here that could contribute to a deterioration in Tim's mental health?
   o What are the grief issues involved and how might they be shaping Tim's behaviour and emotional responses?
   o Was he traumatized by the loss? If so, what are the implications of this for his mental health?
   o Has his mental distress been 'medicalized'? If so, what difference might this make to how he perceives the challenges he is facing and the potential solutions?
   o What is the legal position if his mental state makes him a danger to himself or others?

Again, this is just a small selection of the knowledge base issues that can arise, reflecting once again that we are dealing with complex issues. Trying to address this situation without having our professional knowledge base to fall back on would make for a very difficult undertaking – much more difficult than it needs to be – and one where we could again do more than harm than good if we are not careful.

There are, of course, many more examples I could give, but these should be sufficient to highlight: (i) the key point made in Section 3 that our theory base is a vitally important foundation of understanding; and (ii) we need to draw on that knowledge base as appropriate to make sense of each of the situations we find ourselves in – that is, we need to *theorize* practice. The knowledge base provides the raw materials to help us develop a meaningful picture of what we are dealing with.

How, you may be wondering, does the idea of theorizing practice relate to our theme of 'making a difference'? Well, at the very least, drawing on our professional knowledge base can play an important role in trying to ensure that we are not making a *negative* difference – that is, we are not making a bad situation worse. More positively, though, theorizing practice can give us a better platform of understanding on which to base our actions. That does not guarantee that we will be able to make a positive difference, but it does put us in a much stronger, better equipped position to do so.

In addition to giving a better overall understanding and meaningful picture, theorizing practice can also give us important insights about what steps we can take to make a difference. In particular, it can be helpful in setting the scene for using tools or methods from the repertoire available to us. We shall focus on the use of such tools shortly, but first we need to consider the important role of social work processes and skills.

❖❖❖ KEY POINT ❖❖❖

Trying to 'apply theory to practice' has confused and frustrated students and practitioners for many years. The alternative idea of 'theorizing practice' offers a more realistic and user-friendly way of making sure that our practice is informed practice.

Social work processes

At times there are certain procedures that need to be followed (in relation to child protection concerns, for example), but for the most part, how we tackle our cases leaves a great deal of autonomy as to how we proceed. Having that flexibility is a great advantage, given the complexity and variability of the circumstances we are called upon to deal with. However, too much flexibility can mean that our work is unstructured and unfocused. Consequently, there can be distinct benefits to having a clear idea of what processes can be helpful in moving things forward. These are what we are going to focus on now, beginning with interpersonal processes and then moving on to consider 'the helping process', a sequence of different elements of our work.

Interpersonal processes

When people come together for whatever reason they will influence each other. For example, my behaviour and emotional reactions will owe much to the behaviour and emotional reactions of the person(s) I am interacting with and their behaviour and emotional reactions will owe a great deal to mine. Traditionally there has been a heavy emphasis on individuals, as if we operate in isolation, whereas in reality, as it was emphasized to me when I was a student, all action is interaction.

What this means is that there are complex social processes that go on all the time – social rules, manners and customs, for example. Being aware of these, being tuned in to them is an important part of reflective practice, as they will tell us much about what is going on if we pay attention to them. For 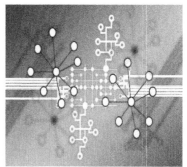 example, in working with a family, we may be able to observe their interactions and get a helpful picture of power relations within that family. This could be in terms of who speaks and who does not, whether disagreements arise and, if so, how they are dealt with.

A powerful dynamic I have witnessed many times in practice is where one person is asked a question, but looks to another family member before answering, as if they are asking permission and/or clarifying the boundaries of what they are allowed to say and what they must remain silent on. It does not take long to pick up on these subtle processes once you know what you are looking for. We shall return to this issue in Section 13 when we examine the significance of nonverbal communication. But, for now, we can see that interpersonal processes are worthy of our attention.

The helping process

In my *People Skills* book (Thompson, 2015b), I describe a process of helping that consists of five elements that operate largely in sequence. These can apply across the human services, but are particularly applicable to social work.

➤ *Assessment* This involves gathering information to form a picture of the situation, including the problems and needs to be addressed and the strengths and resilience factors that need to be taken into consideration and the risk factors involved. This is a crucial part of the process. In my experience, where I have come across examples of social work practice that has gone awry, it is because there was insufficient emphasis on assessment – people started to get involved without first clarifying well enough the nature of the situation they were dealing with. A skimpy assessment can therefore be highly problematic, whereas a good-quality assessment can stand us in very good stead. Sometimes our work ends here, as our assessment may indicate that the person(s) concerned are best signposted elsewhere (the local Citizens' Advice Bureau, for example) or their concerns are not sufficiently serious to warrant professional intervention. Equally, the referral may have been inappropriate or it can perhaps be dealt with there and then. However, in other cases, the assessment leads to further action, and that is where intervention comes in.

➤ *Intervention* Having clarified the situation we are in and formed a picture of what needs doing, intervention is what comes next. That is, once we know what needs doing, we can start doing it. That may involve using a particular tool or method (see later in this Section), developing an approach specific to the particular circumstances or providing (or commissioning) one or more services. We should, however, be wary of the distorting influence of a consumerist approach to social work that has led many people to think narrowly of the social work role as being primarily or exclusively one of providing or commissioning services, with little or no room for direct, problem-solving interventions (see my *The Professional Social Worker* book for a fuller discussion of this common mistake – Thompson, 2016c).

➢ *Review* Assessment is not a one-off activity; we need to keep coming back to it (it is an 'iterative process', to use the technical term). This is because: (i) no assessment is ever 100% complete; there will always be elements of a situation we are not aware of that may subsequently come to light and/or we may become aware that we missed (or misunderstood) something first time round; and (ii) circumstances will change over time, of course; what was the case may no longer be the case now. This is where review comes in. Every so often we need to review the situation, partly to make sure that we are still on track and partly to take into consideration what may have changed. Sometimes – often, in fact – we can get so close to a situation that we cannot see the wood for the trees. Periodic review can therefore guard against this. Review can also enable us to see whether what we are doing is actually working, and, if not, consider what we need to do about it, what changes we might need to make.

➢ *Ending* I have come across many social work textbooks, module descriptors and training courses that cover social work processes issues that make no reference to ending our role (or termination as it is sometimes called). We therefore need to make sure that we do not make the same mistake and lose sight of the need to bear ending in mind. If we are to take seriously values issues around empowerment and avoiding dependency creation, then we should not assume that our involvement will be open ended. Indeed, as one of the tutors used to say when I was a social work student, we should be working towards making ourselves redundant, in the sense of trying to help people manage their own issues wherever possible so that they no longer need us.

➢ *Evaluation* When we bring a piece of work to a close we may be tempted to rush on to the next one or focus more on our other cases. However, if we do this, we are missing out an important step in the process, namely to evaluate how things went. This is for two reasons: (i) in this age of evidence-based practice and the importance of being clear about what works and what does not, it is wise to have evidence, where possible, that what we do actually works, that it does indeed make a positive difference, and so failing to evaluate our work puts us in a weak position in this regard; and (ii) there is so much to learn from examining what worked well and what was not so positive, so that next time we can do even better. Again, this is part of what reflective practice is all about, as we shall see when we get to Section 10.

What we need to be clear about is that these processes need to be undertaken in *partnership* (see Section 6) as far as possible – that is, they are mainly what we do *with* the people we serve and support, rather than *to* them or *about* them.

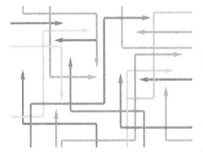

So, whether we are talking about interpersonal processes or the various processes that are part of the helping process, it is essential that we are tuned in to how processes work and what impact they make. We will be missing out on some really important stuff if we lose sight of the myriad processes that are constantly going on in social life in general and in social work in particular.

Social work skills

Social work, it needs to be recognized, is a highly skilled occupation. Many of these are 'people skills' that we share with other professional groups within the human services. Others are specific to social work or largely so – for example, writing reports that focus on the key social work issues involved in a particular case.

We constantly draw on everyday skills, like communicating effectively. However, for professional purposes, we need to be able to take those skills to a more advanced level. For example, if we return to the point made earlier that we need to be tuned in to the processes that are going on around us, even young children can do that much of the time (often better than adults whose heads are full of other issues and concerns). However, if we are to achieve the best results possible as practitioners, then we need to be able demonstrate those skills at a far more advanced level than ordinary people can. This is because ordinarily people can get by quite well without tuning in to certain processes, but in social work we can be oblivious to highly important issues if we do not pick up on the signals around us, if we do not recognize the dynamics involved. For example, in working with an older person, there may be processes going on that suggest that elder abuse is taking place. People engaging with the older person concerned in an everyday way may not suspect at all that abuse is occurring, but it is to be hoped that a trained social worker would pick up on any indicators of abuse if apparent. Of course, this relies on having a knowledge of indicators of elder abuse in the first place, and thereby illustrates one of the important connections between knowledge and skills.

In *People Skills* I divide the skills covered there into three sections or categories (while acknowledging that there will be some overlap across categories – they are not totally separate domains). It is worth revisiting these here:

➢ *Self-management skills* Some jobs place significant physical demands on staff (working on a building site, for example). Social work places a great deal of psychological pressure on its practitioners (and managers), especially emotional pressures (Howe, 2008). What is called for, then is a set of self-management skills – self-awareness and self-care, time and workload management and so on. To put it in simple terms, if we struggle to get our own act together, how can we possibly be effective in helping other people to get their act together when they are distressed, in difficulties or otherwise in need of our help and support.

➢ *Interpersonal skills* So much of what we do involves interacting with other people (whether face to face, by telephone or in writing), and so we need to have the required skills to make these interactions successful – hence the need, as mentioned earlier, for: (i) awareness of, and sensitivity to, interpersonal processes; and (ii) an advanced level of skill well beyond the basic ones we learn as part of our upbringing. It is a matter of becoming an advanced-level communicator and not settling for everyday levels of communicative competence that will only take us so far.

➤ *Intervention skills* Both self-management skills and interpersonal skills are part of what is involved in 'making a difference', but with intervention skills, making a difference is the primary focus. Putting plans into action, keeping a clear focus on what we are doing, using tools and methods – these are all important intervention skills, the skills involved in taking the steps we need. With this in mind we now turn our attention to the question of using tools and methods.

Social work tools

So, we are able to draw on our professional knowledge base to make sense of the situation we are dealing with; we have tuned in to the processes operating and we  are aware of the need to begin with a good-quality assessment to guide us through the helping process; we are aware of the skills we need and we are working hard to build them up and take them to a more advanced level with each day that passed. But now what do we do? What can we draw on to bring about the changes that have been identified in the assessment. This is where the idea of social work tools or methods comes in.

We are fortunate to have a wide range of such tools and methods at our disposal. For example, de Mőnnink's *The Social Workers' Toolbox: Sustainable Multimethod Social Work* contains an impressive array of social work methods together with guidance on when and how to use them (de Mőnnink, 2017). Paul Stepney and I have also co-edited a book that covers a range of social work methods and also discusses the significance of using such methods in practice (Thompson and Stepney, 2018). In addition, my own *People Solutions Sourcebook* contains 88 problem-solving tools and a discussion of how such tools can be used in practice (Thompson, 2012a). Clearly, then, there is no shortage of tools to draw upon.

As with tools in the concrete, physical sense, they will not do the job for you, but they can be very helpful when it comes to making a difference. The parallel with physical tools also extends to the importance of choosing your tools carefully and making sure you are using the right one for the job. You would create more problems than you solve if, for example, you were to use a hammer to insert screws, rather than make use of a screwdriver. Likewise, I remember having a conversation with a student on placement who was telling me that she was using crisis intervention and it was not working. Subsequent discussion revealed that it was not working because the client was not in crisis. She was distressed and struggling, but she had not reached crisis point, so it was no wonder that 'crisis intervention' was proving to be ineffective. It was the wrong tool at the wrong time. The use of tools and methods therefore needs to be underpinned by knowledge (as well as skills and values).

Tools and methods can be very useful, but they have to be used with care and skill. Don't be afraid to try things out, but make sure you have read about what you are planning to use and, where possible, get advice and guidance from someone experienced in using that particular method.

So, to sum up, when it comes to making a difference, what it boils down to is:

- *Theorizing practice* – drawing on our professional knowledge base to help us make sense of the complex situations we find ourselves in.
- *Social work processes* – being tuned in to the various processes that are at work so that we can shape those processes in a positive direction as far as we can.
- *Social work skills* – taking our everyday skills to a more advanced level and learning some new ones along the way.
- *Social work tools* – being aware of the tools and methods available to us, learning more about how to use them and benefiting from what they have to offer.

Tools and Methods Exercise

What tools or methods are you aware of? Make a list below and, for each one, think about what circumstances you might use that particular tool in. What would the factors be that helped you decide when a particular tool of method would be appropriate?

5. Thinking holistically

Sadly, 'holistic' is an overused word. It is often used vaguely and in ambiguous ways. So, let's be entirely clear about the sense in which I am using it here. It refers to looking at the big picture, taking account of wider issues and how they are affecting the situation. It is the opposite of being atomistic which means focusing narrowly on individualistic factors as if the wider context does not matter. So, the message of being holistic is: the wider context does indeed matter and we are relying on a distorted picture if we do not consider it.

Consequently, in this section we are going to explore the relevance of various aspects of the wider context in which social work takes place and in which citizens live their lives.

HOLISTIC
Takes account of the individual *and* the wider context

ATOMISTIC
Focuses narrowly on the individual and neglects the wider context

The organizational context

Some social workers operate independently on a self-employed basis, but the vast majority are employees of an organization, often a large organization. On the plus side, this means that there will be access to resources and colleagues and managers to back us up when needed (in principle at least). However, there is also the downside that organizations will have their own problems and challenges. Sadly, organizational life can create barriers to high-quality practice. This includes in the following ways:

➤ *A narrow focus on targets* For many organizations targets and performance indicators are a fact of life that can't be ignored or bypassed, however problematic or unrealistic such targets may be. It takes quite a management skill (or set of skills) to making sure the targets are met (because the penalties for not doing so can be severe), while also ensuring high-quality practice takes place.

➤ *Work overload* One of the common consequences of a narrow focus on targets is excessive workloads (although this is not the only cause). Excessive workloads can lead to a vicious circle: the more overloaded someone is, the more they struggle; the more they struggle, the less they achieve; the less they achieve, the more anxious they get; the more anxious they get, the more they struggle; the more they struggle, the less they achieve; and so on. We shall return to the question of managing a heavy workload in Section 27.

➤ *Organizational culture* Organizational cultures are sets of habits, taken-for-granted assumptions and unwritten rules that have a very powerful effect on organizational life. All organizations have them, and large organizations can also have a set of subcultures (in different teams and sections). Cultures can be helpful or harmful (or have some helpful elements and some harmful ones). Because of this it becomes important to be aware of the key elements of the culture you work in so that you are in a stronger position to capitalize on the positives and tackle the negatives as far as possible. Sadly, some people become 'culture victims' – that is, they just follow the culture unthinkingly and uncritically. So, if there is a culture characterized by poor communication and poor practice, some people will limit their communication and settle for poor-quality practice, so that they feel more comfortable 'fitting in'. This is, of course, a dangerous strategy to adopt, albeit a common one.

➤ *Level of morale* The terms 'motivation' and 'morale' are often used interchangeably, but they are actually quite different. Motivation is an individual, psychological phenomenon, whereas morale is a sociological phenomenon – it is about *shared* levels of motivation, commitment and engagement. In this respect, it is an aspect of organizational culture. It is also a reflection of the quality of leadership. It is important to understand morale as social because a low morale culture can operate as if it is infectious. For example, a highly motivated individual joining a team with low morale is likely to be dragged down by the culture. It is therefore important to be able to *transcend* a culture – that is, go beyond it, not simply be a passive victim of it – especially a low morale culture.

➤ *Teamwork* Effective teamwork can make a hugely positive difference to quality of work, to quality of working life and to organizational success. Poor or non-existent teamwork, by contrast, can be highly destructive. A common mistake is to assume that the quality of teamwork is the responsibility of the team leader or manager, whereas, in reality, it is the responsibility of each and every member of the team. It is then the responsibility of the team leader or manager to make sure that everyone plays their part.

It is very easy for these important organizational factors to just fade into the background and just become 'wallpaper' that we don't notice. The more this happens, the more likely we are to become passive victims of important organizational dynamics that can have a highly significant impact on the quality of our practice, our level of motivation, our learning and development, our effectiveness and our job satisfaction. Those people who bury themselves in their organization and pay it no attention are therefore missing out on a great deal and leaving themselves quite vulnerable to the negative aspects of organizational life.

The legal and policy context

While, as social workers, we have a certain degree of professional autonomy, we are none the less constrained by wider contextual factors, not least the legislative framework and the social and organizational policies that flow from them. We therefore need to be aware of those wider legal and policy issues if we are not to find ourselves in considerable difficulties. Whole textbooks have been written about (i) social work law; and (ii) social policy, so I am not going to summarize the key elements here. Instead, I am going to concentrate on emphasizing four key points that we need to make sure that we do not lose sight of:

➢ *Ignorance is no excuse* Social workers are not expected to be legal experts, but we do need to know at least the basics of the law relating to: (i) social work

 issues in general (human rights, for example); and (ii) our particular area of practice (children's legislation or mental health law, for example). We also need to know how and where to find out more as the need arises and be prepared to seek support and guidance where required. The same applies to social policy – we need at the very least a basic understanding of relevant social policy (in relation to the philosophy behind community care, for example) and be prepared to learn more where needed.

➢ *Law and policy provide a framework for action* In my time I have encountered a good many people who see law and policy as something to be feared or at least resented, not recognizing just how useful these matters can be as a guide to action. Of course, they will not tell us exactly what to do, and nor should they, but they will provide a structure and a basis for planning. Indeed, a useful starting point when undertaking an assessment is to ask ourselves: What does the law say about matters like this? How does this situation fit into the social policy context?

➢ *Law and policy empower as well as constrain* The law gives us certain powers as well as duties; it opens some doors while closing others. It is therefore essential that we do not have too negative a view of law and policy as if they are bugbears we have to contend with. In reality, they are very useful tools that can provide us with positive ways forward in dealing with complex and demanding situations.

➤ *Confidence is paramount* I have already emphasized the crucial role of confidence in preparing ourselves for high-quality practice. This applies in particular to matters relating to law and policy. In Section 18 we shall explore the demands of court work as part of social work practice, and that can, of course, understandably be seen as a potential source of anxiety. However, I have also come across many situations where people feel anxious and unconfident in dealing with law and policy issues more broadly. This is no doubt because they fear getting things wrong and thereby potentially facing public censure. However, the irony here is that the less confident we are, the greater the chance of getting something wrong and therefore the greater the chance of facing public censure. By contrast, the more confident we are (subjectively), the more credibility we will have and the more effective we can be (and the more justified we can feel in having our subjective confidence, our self-belief).

Once again it is the case that, the more knowledgeable we are of the wider context – in this case, the legal and policy context – the stronger we will be when it comes to rising to the many significant challenges we face in social work.

The social context

A key value in social work is the need to be non-judgemental. Part of the reason for this is that it is an easy mistake to make to make negative value judgements about people without knowing their story, without knowing what hand life has dealt them. Consider the following examples:

- The man who seems to wallow in self-pity and keeps being told to 'pull himself together' has had multiple serious losses in his life and has been left feeling devastated, abandoned and beyond hope. Failing to offer him help (or helping him less enthusiastically) because he 'doesn't help himself' would simply add to his sense of abandonment and hopelessness – we have become part of the problem, rather than part of the solution.

- The woman who is seen as having 'loose morals' because she has five children from five different fathers was regularly raped by her step-father between the ages of 11 and 16, an experience that means she finds it extremely difficult to trust men and remain in a relationship with them. It also means that she gets a great sense of pride and satisfaction from being a protective and loving mother. Accepting other people's dismissal of her as a 'slag' fails to recognize her strengths and her resilience.

- The child who really pushes the barriers of acceptable behaviour and creates havoc is operating on the principle that 'if you are not strong enough to control me, you are not strong enough to protect me'. Labelling him or her as a 'problem child' or medicalizing their problem with a diagnosis then prevents us from finding out what does he or she need protecting from. We fail to see that a child who *causes* problems is normally a child who *has* problems, and we thereby fail to offer the hand of protection.

I could go on adding example after example, but the point that I want to emphasize is that the pitfalls of being judgemental stem from failing to recognize the significance of the wider social context. If we see people in isolation (atomism), rather than holistically, then we will fail to note the impact of wider social factors like poverty, alienation, discrimination, oppression, exclusion, abuse and exploitation and so on. As I have put it so many times before, we should never forget why the term 'social worker' begins with the word 'social'.

*** KEY POINT ***

Judgemental attitudes are a very common feature of social life. However, in social work, we need to get past these, as they will stand in the way of effective – and ethical – practice. Bearing in mind the impact of the social context on people's lives can help us to do this.

However, we should beware one common misunderstanding. Being non-judgemental does not mean that we should attempt to justify actions that are harmful or otherwise unacceptable. Rather, it is a case of, as it was helpfully put to me when I was a social work student, condemn the behaviour, not the person.

The political context

Politics is about the exercise of power; democratic politics is nominally in the interests of the people, although it would be naïve not to recognize that other interests (big business, for example) do not also play a part. It would also be naïve not to recognize that political factors also have a significant impact on social work, not least through shaping the legal and policy context discussed above. For example, I have had many conversations with social workers who were critical of their managers' emphasis on targets as if this were a personal failing somehow, rather than a reflection of the wider political issues of managerialism that are part of the politics and economics of neoliberalism that are currently so dominant (Thompson, 2017b).

Politics can be seen to apply at (at least) three levels:

➢ *International* Politics is a global enterprise, in the sense that what happens in one country can have an effect on many other countries. From a social work perspective, consider the significance of refugees and the social needs that become apparent when a large number of refugees enter a country. International politics can also have an impact on levels of employment and other such social issues.

➢ *National* In the UK this subdivides into political issues that apply across the whole UK and those that relate specifically to the four nations within the UK. Initiatives at each of these national levels will, of course, have a strong bearing on funding levels, priorities, the relationship between social work and other human services (health care, for example) and so on.

➤ *Local* Local government in many countries plays a central role in how social work is organized, delivered, resourced, supported and publicized. Local authorities will generally have their own policies that are designed to meet the requirements of national (and/or international) policies and associated legal frameworks.

International

National

Local

These are the main broad three levels, although there will also be some countries that vary from this – for example, by having a regional level of government.

We should note that this is how governmental politics works, but there will also be other 'layers' of politics to consider. This would include: organizational politics (power plays within teams, especially the senior management team, for example); interdisciplinary politics (relations between social work and health care staff, for example); community politics (differing agendas across community leaders, for example); and family politics (power dynamics within and between families, for example).

Clearly, then, political factors are all around us. It is therefore important that we do not make the mistake of thinking that we can 'just get on with the job' and take no notice of the wider political context. Politics is about power, and if we are paying little or no attention to it, then we run the risk of being victims of that power and allowing the people we serve and support to lose out.

The historical context

Compassion, humanitarianism and helping and supporting others can be traced back to ancient times, but where it becomes possible to say that 'social work' began is a contentious issue and one with differing schools of thought. But, putting that debate to one side, we can certainly recognize that social work has been around for some time. It has had its ups and downs, its victories and defeats and, of course it has evolved in different ways in different countries and different settings.

It is perhaps worth sharing the wisdom of philosopher, George Santayana (1863-1952), who argued that those who pay no attention to their history are doomed to repeat its mistakes (Santayana, 2013). We have a rich and fascinating history in social work and much to be proud of. Disconnecting ourselves from our history by wanting to 'just get on with the job' is therefore very unwise.

We should therefore remember to include the historical context in our consideration of how significant the broader context is in shaping people's lives, their problems, the potential solutions and the opportunities for empowerment.

Thinking Holistically Exercise

What problems are likely to arise if we do not think holistically? What could go wrong if we just focused narrowly on the individual and/or family and paid no heed to the wider contextual factors discussed in this section?

6. Working in partnership

Social work is what we do *with* people, not *to* them is one of the lessons I learned from my first placement as a social work student, and that wisdom has stayed with me throughout my career. In those days it wasn't called working in partnership; that is a more recent term that has emerged, but the idea is fundamentally the same.

In this section we are going to look at what working in partnership actually means in practice. We will look at three different, but related, facets of partnership: with clients, with carers and with fellow professionals.

With clients

There are three different, but connected reasons for working in partnership. First, in some cases at least, there is a legal requirement that we work in partnership. Second, there is a pragmatic reason, in the sense that experience has taught us that we can make more effective progress in bringing about change if we work together as partners, rather than try to impose change on people (imposed change is widely recognized as the least effective form of change). But third, and perhaps most importantly, there is a moral reason for working in partnership. What right have we to do things *to* people, before first trying to work *with* them? As social workers, we have power, and with this comes an ethical duty to exercise any such authority responsibly. We would be hard pushed to justify using authority when it was not necessary, when we could have worked together voluntarily. Of course, there will be some situations where we do have to exercise authority, but that should be a last resort. Why try to coerce someone into doing something they would be happy to do willingly if handled properly (that is, skilfully and sensitively). We should therefore understand partnership as a social work value, as well as a practice tool.

So, what does working in partnership with clients look like in practice? In courses I have run on the subject I have emphasized four key elements, the Four Cs (Thompson, 2018a):

➤ *Clarity and agreement about goals* We need to be clear about why we are in the life of this person (family, group or community). What is our role? As we discussed in Section 1, confusion about this can cause problems and erect barriers. In Section 23 we shall see why it is important to focus on outcomes, to be systematic in our approach, so that there is clarity about what we are working towards. Without this sense of purpose we can find ourselves at sea, with no clarity about how best to proceed. Part of our assessment therefore needs to be the process of establishing aims and objectives. Working in partnership means that we need to ensure that these are *shared* aims and

 objectives – that is, there is agreement about what outcomes (desired end results) we are working towards. For example, in a situation where is an unacceptably high level of risk, there needs to be an agreement that one outcome to work towards is to reduce the level of risk to the

point where it becomes acceptable. Clearly, then, there is a degree of negotiation involved. Indeed, negotiation skills can be seen as an essential basis for working in partnership, whether with clients or anyone else. If there is no agreement about where we are trying to get to, then it is highly unlikely that we will get there.

➤ *Clarity and agreement about how to achieve the goals (agreed strategies of intervention)* Having established agreement about what is to be achieved, about what we are working towards, we now need to establish agreement about *how* we are going to be able to achieve them, about what steps we need to take to get us there. Sometimes that will be relatively simple and straightforward, but it can also be a highly challenging process that requires a lot of skill. Some people will want to resist any effort to address the issues involved due to anxiety or for various other reasons. In other circumstances, the client may want a simple answer to a complex set of issues, and we may need to persuade them of the difficulties involved in that course of action. To counterbalance these challenges, though, we should also recognize that things will often go very smoothly, especially if we have done a good job of establishing agreement about what we are trying to achieve together and thereby established a helpful degree of trust and credibility.

➢ *Conflict management skills* When we get to Section 20 we will look closely at the question of conflict management. The subject deserves a whole section of its own because it is such a common feature of social work practice (and yet so often neglected in social work education and training). I mentioned the role of negotiation skills earlier, and they can be seen as part of conflict management in terms of both preventing it and addressing it when it does arise. When it comes to working in partnership there can be disagreements (and thus conflict) about what needs to be achieved and/or how it is to be achieved. In the former case, it may be, for example, that a mother living with someone who has a criminal record for abusing children does not appreciate the risk involved to her children ('That was ages ago, he's changed since then. He wouldn't hurt a fly'), while child protection procedures require us to pay much fuller attention to the risks involved. Likewise, someone with a serious drink or drugs problem may not appreciate how problematic their behaviour has become. In terms of disagreement about how to tackle the problems or needs identified, a common source of difficulties arises from the prevalence of 'consumerist' expectations – that is, people may have expectations that the answer to their problem is to have a service provided, when there are other steps that can be taken to address the needs without recourse to providing or commissioning a service (for example, work undertaken to address family tensions relating to adolescent behaviour with a view to avoiding reception into care, even though the view of the parent(s) is that being 'put away' is the answer). We shall discuss the problems associated with consumerism in Section 24.

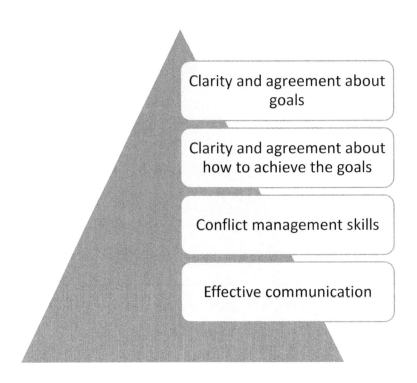

> *Effective and appropriate communication* Of course, one of the main ways of managing conflict is through effective and appropriate communications (as we shall see in Section 20, problems with communication are often at the root of conflict situations). However, the importance of effective communication extends far beyond conflict management. Indeed, we need to be aware that communication is at the heart of partnership working. Poor or non-existent communication is certainly no foundation for effective partnership. We therefore need to be very clear about what needs to be communicated and make sure that such communication takes place appropriately and in a timely manner. This applies to communication in writing as well, of course. Keeping people in the dark, verbally or in writing, can undo a lot of good work and place us in a very weak position when it comes to clarifying aims and objectives and how we are going to work together to achieve them. We shall return to this theme in Section 13.

With carers

Sadly, the needs of carers can often be allowed to slip out of the picture. Informal carers (family members, neighbours, friends and so on) can be under immense pressure in terms of the demands of caring for someone they care about.

Likewise, paid carers face a difficult and demanding job which, if it is to be carried out properly, relies on having proper information and clear plans to work to. So, in both cases, partnership is an important issue, in the sense that all involved in providing care need to be 'on the same page' and totally clear about needs to be done and what is not to be done.

Consequently, much of what has already been said in relation to partnership with clients also applies to working in partnership with carers: clarity about what is to be achieved and how; effective and appropriate communication; and effective conflict management. This last issue is particularly important. This is because:

➢ We should not assume that the relationship between carer and cared for is an entirely harmonious and positive one. There may be conflicts and tension, and these will often be kept out of sight of 'outsiders', including the social worker. We therefore need to be tuned in to the possibility of any such conflicts or tensions and be alert to any tell-tale signs (for example, as revealed in body language). In some cases, such tensions could actually amount to abuse. Unfortunately, in some circumstances the pressures of caring can evoke an abusive response. In addition, there may have been pre-existing tensions before the caregiving relationship began. For example, I recall dealing with a situation where an elderly man who had become dependent on his wife for his day-to-day care and who was being treated very harshly by her. The reason why became apparent when she confided in me that, before he became incapacitated, he had been physically and emotionally abusive towards her on a regular basis.

➢ There may be a conflict between what has been agreed between social worker and client about what needs to be achieved and how, but the carer may not agree. If the disagreement is openly voiced, it can be discussed and appropriate negotiations take place. However, what is much more difficult is if the disagreement is kept secret for whatever reason, as that can easily result in plans being foiled by the actions, inactions and/or attitudes of the carer. This can be deliberate sabotage for whatever reason, but it can also arise from genuine concern. For example, a carer who is impatient to get an elderly relative who has had a fall back to normal as soon as possible may rush the rehabilitation plan and risk making the situation worse.

> ➤ There may at times be resentment on the part of some carers that there is a social worker involved, a professional who is now, as it were, invading their territory. In my own practice I often had to 'win over' carers to convince them that professional help was needed, as they seemed to see such help as a sign that they had failed, that they were inadequate in some way.

It should be clear, then, that working in partnership with carers has much in common with partnership work with clients, but with some extra issues to take account of.

>>> **Moccasins moment** <<<

If you were in a caregiving role and a social worker became involved, what would you expect from him or her in terms of making a reality of the idea that they would be working in partnership with you? How would this partnership manifest itself in concrete terms?

With fellow professionals

Multidisciplinary collaboration is the reality for much of social work practice, but it can also be quite a challenge. This is because different professionals will often have different:

- Roles;
- Plans;
- Priorities;
- Pressures;
- Perspectives;
- Values; and

- Education and training.

For example, a nurse working with a disabled person who is struggling to cope alone in the community and is at considerable risk in terms of health and well-being, may see their role in terms of making him or her safe by recommending residential care. By contrast, a social worker, while alert to the risk involved, may also be concerned with safeguarding the client's right to self-determination and to live at risk if he or she chooses to do so.

Equally, different professionals may not appreciate each other's pressures and constraints. I once ran a Diploma in Child Protection course in which half the participants were social workers and half were health care professionals. It emerged from this course that each group had little understanding of the  other group's circumstances. For example, the social workers were amazed to find out how many families health visitors had on their books and could see now that their expectations of how much input into a child protection case a health visitor could make were unrealistic. By the same token, the health care staff were surprised to learn that social workers had no right of entry into people's homes and that they could not remove a child from harm without a court order.

What these issues illustrate is that multidisciplinary partnership can easily go wrong if people are not aware of, and sensitive to, the different circumstances that the other staff groups find themselves in. It is ironic that some social workers who are rightly keen not to be judgemental towards clients will readily allow themselves to be judgemental towards fellow professionals and not take the trouble to try and see the situation from their point of view. We will return to this point in Section 20 where we focus on conflict management.

What can also be part of this situation is that many people, including many fellow professionals, do not have a good understanding of the social work role and its limits.

People generally know what nurses, teachers and police officers do, but, unless they have direct experience (and perhaps not even then), they may not appreciate what social workers do (and do not do). It is therefore essential that we develop the skills of 'setting out our stall'. By this I mean being able to explain clearly and effectively what we can do and what we cannot do – that is, to provide a helpful and accurate picture of the extent of our role and therefore its limits. If we do not actually do this, there is a very real danger that they will have a limited understanding or, worse still, a distorted understanding of our role, and that, of course, can cause a great deal of difficulty, not least by wrecking the potential for effective partnership working.

Whichever type of partnership you are trying to establish (with clients, with carers or with fellow professionals) it is essential that you develop the skills necessary for *setting out your stall* – that is, clarifying expectations for the benefit of all. Without this, things can easily go badly wrong.

Why partnership?

Why should we work in partnership? Why don't we just get on with the job and leave others to get on with their job and to live their lives as they see fit? There are, in fact, several reasons, including:

- Imposed change is the least effective change, as mentioned earlier, so working in partnership is more effective, as well as being more ethically appropriate.

- There is also the 'Gestalt effect' as captured by the saying that the whole is greater than the sum of its parts – that is, we can achieve more by working together than by working apart.

- There is a danger that people's needs may fall between two (or more) stools – that is, if the different people involved are not communicating properly, a client's or carer's needs may not be met.

- Without effective partnership we may not be getting the whole picture (consider the importance in safeguarding situations of all the professionals involved sharing information in order to 'piece together the jigsaw').

- There is also the issue of potential inequality of access and outcome – that is, unfairness may creep in if do not have the full picture to work with; someone whose needs are lesser than someone else's may get a service, for example, while the person with the greater need does not.

The case for partnership working should therefore be fairly well established, so we need to make sure that we never lose sight of just how important it is or allow it to become something that is just paid lip service to.

One of the main benefits of working in partnership is that it is a firm basis for promoting equality and valuing diversity, and so it is to these issues that we will turn next in Section 7. But first, don't forget to complete the Working in Partnership exercise and record your reflections below for future reference (as well as to consolidate your understanding of the key issues).

Working in Partnership Exercise

What obstacles to working in partnership can think of? List as many as you can (with the help of colleagues if you wish). What steps might you be able to take to avoid, remove or get past these obstacles or to minimize their impact?

7. Equality, diversity and social justice

A commitment to anti-discriminatory practice has long featured as an expectation of all social workers in the UK and in many places beyond. A huge amount has been written and spoken about it over the decades, some it very helpful, some of it less so. The issues involved are very complex and often sensitive, and, sadly efforts to tackle the issues involved have often been plagued by a tendency towards oversimplification (trying to find simple solutions to complex issues is rarely, if ever, a wise move) and no small amount of in-fighting across different interest groups.

Despite these problems, the need to challenge discrimination and the oppression it leads to has managed to remain widely recognized, albeit not as fully as once the case. So, we should be glad that, despite the stormy times over the years, we have retained a strong awareness of the extent to which our clientele is highly prone to being discriminated against. If you think carefully about it, you will no doubt quickly realize that most, if not all, of the groups of people we support in social work are liable to be discriminated against. If you add to that the fact that there are also issues of racism and sexism that apply across the board in society and not just to specific client groups, it becomes apparent that discrimination and oppression are major factors that we need to take account of — hence the focus in this section on equality, diversity and social justice.

I shall comment on each of these three sets of issues (equality, diversity and social justice) in turn and then highlight some pitfalls to avoid and some principles of good practice.

Equality and difference

Equality in its literal sense means sameness (2 + 2 = 4 means two plus two is the same as four). Unfortunately, many people have used it in this literal sense when applying it to issues around professional values. Consequently, for a long time there was a common saying along the lines of: 'We believe in equality, we believe in treating everybody the same'. We rarely hear that these days but the idea that equality means sameness is still quite common. This is an example of the oversimplification I referred to earlier. If we treat everybody the same, we simply reinforce existing inequalities. For example, if we treat black people the same as we treat white people, we are, in effect, ignoring the significance of racism. Equality, then, is not about sameness, it is about fairness, treating people with equal fairness. Often, treating people fairly will amount to treating everybody the same, but there will also be times when the needs of an individual or group are such that it is fair to treat them differently – for example, it is fair to treat children differently from adults because children have different needs and circumstances.

If we were to make the mistake of thinking of equality as sameness, then equality and diversity would be opposites and incompatible with one another. If, however, we see equality as being about equal fairness, then we can see that equality and diversity are entirely compatible and supportive of one another. Diversity is about valuing difference and equality is about making sure that difference is not used as a reason for treating someone unfairly (that is discriminating against them). Equality can therefore be understood as the absence of unfair discrimination – not about treating everybody the same, but about making sure that differences are respected and valued, rather than used as the basis for oppressing particular individuals, groups or categories of people.

It needs to be recognized that these are complex and sensitive issues, and so a sophisticated level of understanding is called for, meaning that we need to approach such matters in a spirit of critically reflective practice.

Difference and diversity

I made the point earlier that diversity involves valuing difference. Literally, diversity means variety, and this raises three important issues:

1. We need to recognize that we live and work in a diverse society. Experience has taught me that many people have a very blinkered view of society and seem to overestimate the extent of uniformity across peoples. For example, on training courses I have run I have asked participants if they know how many different languages are spoken in their county or borough. In every single case, their estimates have been far lower than the reality.

2. We also need to recognize that diversity is a good thing, an asset, not a problem – hence the idea of valuing diversity or even of celebrating diversity. Life would be highly problematic if everyone were the same, with the same tastes, opinions, approaches, priorities, interests and ambitions. Variety enriches our society.

3. Unfortunately, however, some people see diversity as a problem. They regard people who are perceived as 'different' as either inferior or a threat (or both).

4. This is the basis of discrimination. In its literal sense, to discriminate is to identify a difference, and is clearly something we need to do in our lives (for example, to differentiate between what is safe and what is dangerous). However, while discriminating *between* is a useful thing to do, the problems arise when we discriminate *against*. That refers to when we not only identify certain people as different from ourselves in some way(s), but also go a step further in regarding that difference as a justification for treating them less favourably (excluding them, stigmatizing them, denying them rights and, in some cases, even attacking them) – in other words, oppressing them.

*** KEY POINT ***

Anti-discriminatory practice rests on challenging the idea that difference is a justification for less favourable treatment, hence the emphasis on valuing diversity.

Discrimination and social justice

Traditionally discrimination has been understood as an individualistic matter, a reflection of personal prejudice, for example. However, a key feature of my work over the years has been the challenging of this oversimplified approach to the issues (Thompson, 2007; 2016d; 2017a; 2018a). Issues of discrimination and oppression need to be understood not just as psychological matters at the personal level, but also as part of a commitment to social justice. This involves understanding the sociological aspects of discrimination as well as (and not instead of) the psychological elements, hence my emphasis on PCS analysis, the need to understand discrimination in terms of the three levels and the interactions across them:

P – Personal: individual factors relating to how we perceive other people and our relationships with them.

C – Cultural: shared meanings and taken-for-granted assumptions that are part of our upbringing and which are very influential in shaping our perceptions and understandings at a personal level. Such cultural factors are often discriminatory (based on stereotypes, for example, or distorted media representations).

S – Structural: society is not a level playing field; some people are born with certain advantages (inherited wealth, for example), while others are born with certain disadvantages (being a member of an oppressed minority, for example). The power relations (that is, relations of dominance and subordination) at this structural level will play a significant role in shaping the cultural assumptions at the **C** level. It is therefore no coincidence that the discriminatory assumptions at the **C** level that shape to a large extent discriminatory attitudes, behaviour and language at the **P** level are themselves largely shaped by the power relations at the **S** level and, in turn, serve to reinforce them, thereby keeping the wheels of power turning (to the detriment of the least powerful groups and to the benefit of the power elite).

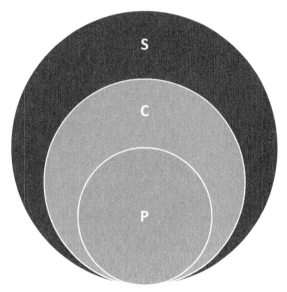

Social justice is about ensuring that all groups and categories of people are treated fairly. It is a counterbalance to cultural and structural forces in society that reinforce advantages for certain groups while discriminating against others. PCS analysis helps us to understand how this operates, so that we are better equipped to recognize discrimination and better placed to tackle it. For example, in working with older people, it can sensitize us to the significance of ageism and give us a framework of what is happening so that we can deal with the issues in a more informed way.

TIP! Bear in mind that PCS analysis is not just something for students to quote in their essays. It is also a useful *practice* tool. It can help us make sense of the complexities involved in issues relating to discrimination and oppression.

Pitfalls to avoid

I have already emphasized that the issues relating to equality, diversity and social justice are complex and sensitive. One of the implications of this is that it is quite easy to get things wrong. Because of this it is important that we are alert to the main pitfalls to avoid, and that is what we are going to focus on here. Please note, though, that this is not a comprehensive or exhaustive list – there are plenty more pitfalls besides the ones listed here!

> *Dogmatic reductionism* This is a technical term that refers to how efforts to promote equality and value diversity have been hijacked by some people whose approach to the issues has been counterproductive. Dogmatic refers to the tendency to adopt a rigid approach, to look for hard and fast rules that are just too inflexible to work in such complex circumstances. Reductionism refers to the tendency to oversimplify complex, multi-level matters to a simple, single-level explanation. A classic example of dogmatic reductionism is the 'political correctness' approach to the relationship between language and discrimination. Simply banning certain words without any explanation or more sophisticated understanding of how language works is a woefully inadequate response to the challenge of tackling discriminatory forms of language. Simply telling people what they can or cannot say is more likely to alienate them than to enlighten them. What is called for is a much more sophisticated understanding of the issues involved, a greater sensitivity to how language works and how it can contribute to (or challenge) discrimination. There is, of course, much more to language than just individual words (that are often taken out of context). See the discussion of political correctness in Thompson (2018b).

> *Defensiveness* The prevalence of dogmatic reductionism at one time led to a hostile, hectoring approach to the issues, characterized by a punitive way of dealing with perceived incidences of discrimination, rather than an educational and empowering one. One of the consequences of this was that a culture of fear developed, and this discouraged people from addressing discrimination and oppression issues, preferring to steer clear of them

wherever possible for fear of having a label of racist, sexist or whatever attached to them. As a result of this, defensive approaches were very common at one time. Thankfully, we have made considerable progress in that regard over the years, but it would be both naïve and unrealistic to think that the problem no longer applies at all. This takes us back to the issue of the importance of confidence. We have to be careful not to be complacent, of course, but an unconfident approach to anti-discriminatory practice is likely to be quite problematic. For example, if our body language gives off a message to the effect that we are not comfortable in dealing with the issues, this could easily be interpreted as a message to the effect that we are not committed to making a positive difference.

> *Essentialism* This is a philosophical term that refers to the mistaken view that people have a fixed personality that cannot be changed: 'That's the way he is; he can't help it' or 'That's her nature; she'll never change' (if people were not capable of change, what would the point of social work be?). This is another process of oversimplification. For example, saying that someone is 'a racist', as if this is some sort of character flaw inherent within them is unnecessarily defeatist. Often people will express racist ideas because they are reflecting their upbringing (and thus their culture at the **C** level), or because they have a limited understanding of the issues involved. People can and do change their attitudes and behaviours (although this is not to say that everyone is *willing* to change their attitude), so presenting their discriminatory characteristics as fixed and unchangeable is both unhelpful and inaccurate.

There is much more that could be said about pitfalls to avoid, but what I want to emphasize is the need to be alert to the issues, to be 'tuned in'. It is a case of finding a balance between, on the one hand, being anxious and defensive and thereby wanting simple solutions and, on the other, being dangerously complacent by not taking sufficient account of the harm that discrimination and oppression cause, the havoc that they wreak in so many people's lives (bear in mind my earlier point about how common it is for social work client groups to be highly prone to various forms of discrimination).

Principles of good practice

Having looked at some of the pitfalls to be avoided, I'm now going to present the other side of the coin by offering some guidance on principles of good practice. Again, this is not a comprehensive or exhaustive list, but it should none the less be a helpful one.

➤ *Be realistic!* The problems of discrimination and oppression are woven deeply into the fabric of society and hugely complex. In many respects, their roots lie in the structure and organization of wider society and our political and economic systems. This leads some people to be cynical and defeatist about the potential for change, arguing that there is little point trying to address the problems as they are too deeply ingrained. This argument is flawed in (at least) two ways: on the one hand, we can draw a parallel with crime. We could reasonably argue that crime is deeply rooted in the nature of our society and social relations and therefore the idea of a crime-free society is something that will never be achieved. However, it would not follow that we should therefore not bother to have the police, courts, the probation service and so on, as crime is 'inevitable'. Similarly, arguing that some degree of discrimination is inevitable is certainly no justification for not doing the best we can to keep it to a minimum. On the other hand, it fails to recognize that not addressing discrimination amounts to condoning it. For example, if someone expresses Islamophobic (or other discriminatory) sentiments and these are not challenged, the person concerned is likely to assume that such attitudes are acceptable and unproblematic. We therefore have to steer clear of this cynical defeatism, while also not being naïve enough to think we can rid the world of discrimination through our practice. It is about being realistic about what we can achieve and doing our best to make sure that we achieve it as fully as possible.

➤ *Challenge elegantly* In social work we are likely to come across discrimination on a fairly regular basis. If we ignore it (or become so blasé that we fail to recognize it), we are, as I mentioned just a moment ago, in effect condoning it, giving a message that it is acceptable. It is therefore essential that we challenge discrimination consistently and persistently. However, what arose as part of the dogmatic reductionism problem was a tendency to challenge in a hostile, aggressive way. For example, I was once a guest speaker at a university when a male student made a mildly sexist comment that would have been best handled calmly and sensitively and as a learning opportunity (especially as this was the first week of the course for the new intake of students). However, one of the tutors stood up at that point and said in a harsh, hectoring tone of voice words to the effect of: 'Let's make it quite clear right from the start: that type of oppressive language will not be tolerated on this course'. The result was: (i) acute embarrassment all round; (ii) a rapid end to the discussion I had managed to generate (not an easy feat for me to achieve in a group of 70+ students in the first week of term when the group still did not feel comfortable with each other or with university life); (iii) the foundations laid for a defensive approach for this group of students from here on in; and (iv) a complete lack of credibility for the tutor as an alleged skilled educator. This type of over-the-top challenging is known as 'inelegant' challenging, because it is crude and ill-thought through. What is needed, then, is *elegant* challenging – that is, carefully worded challenges that are designed to help people appreciate why you are objecting and help them to learn about the issues. It is *assertive* challenging geared towards win-win outcomes, rather than an *aggressive* win-lose where the result is likely to be resentment and a possible backlash (as well as a potential hardening of attitudes) – see the discussion of assertiveness in Section 20.

➤ *Keep a focus on values* Not losing sight of our values is wise advice across the board in social work, but when it comes to equality, diversity and social justice, it is especially important that we keep sight of the fact that these are values matters we are dealing with. They are ethical and political concerns which means that, if we are to fulfil our professional duties by acting with integrity (see Section 8), we need to rise to the challenges involved in a spirit of wanting to make a positive difference, not defensively to avoid criticism or out of a sense that it is 'what we are supposed to do'.

One final point to emphasize about anti-discriminatory practice is that the issues are so complex, so sensitive and so fundamental to good practice that we need to keep learning about them. We will never reach the point where we know everything there is to know, partly because of the size and complexity of the field and partly because it is a constantly changing and evolving field. Anti-discriminatory practice is a real challenge to making a reality of the idea of 'continuous professional development'.

>>> Moccasins moment <<<

Imagine that you or your family needed help from a social worker at some point. Imagine that he or she appeared oblivious to issues of potential discrimination and just wanted to 'get on with the job'. How comfortable or safe would you feel in that situation?

Anti-Discriminatory Practice Exercise

What aspects of anti-discriminatory practice do you feel least confident about? Why do they make you feel less confident? What can you do to feel better equipped to address them? Who is the best person to help you with this?

8. Being a professional

Professionalism in social work has a chequered history, in the UK at least. In my *The Professional Social Worker* book (Thompson, 2016c), I trace the history from an elitist 'we know best' professionalism that did not sit comfortably with social work values through a period of 'anti-professionalism' influenced by radical social work's rejection of professionalism (rather than the rejection of elitism) on to a long period of confusion as to whether social work is or is not a profession, right through to the current emphasis on 'authentic professionalism'. I will clarify below what is meant by authentic professionalism and explain why it is important. However, before I do that, I want to look at some of the key elements of professionalism and consider their implications for actual practice. This practice emphasis is important, as there is a tendency on the part of some people at least to see professionalism as an abstract entity far removed from the day-to-day reality of practice which fails to recognize that professionalism –authentic professionalism – is at the heart of good practice.

The alternatives

I am going to cover seven key aspects of professionalism before returning to the question of authentic professionalism, but first it is important to consider the alternatives to professionalism and, in so doing, establish why professionalism is an essential aspect of practice for us to consider. So, what are the alternatives to professionalism? Let's consider the three main ones:

➢ *Being unprofessional* Consider for a moment what it means to be 'unprofessional'. It is clearly not a good thing to be. As we look at the seven dimensions of professionalism we will be able to see that an absence of any one of them is likely to be highly problematic and could potentially put us in considerable difficulties (not least in terms of our credibility or objective confidence).

➤ *Being amateurish* 'Amateur' comes from the Latin word for to love, so an amateur is someone who loves what they do. In that sense, being an amateur is a good thing. However, that is clearly not the whole story, as being described as 'amateurish' would not generally be seen as complimentary. Being amateurish means not taking your responsibilities seriously and/or not being able to function at a high enough level to do your job properly. Given that being able to influence people in a positive direction is a key part of social work, being perceived as amateurish is likely to be a major obstacle to progress.

➤ *Being bureaucratic* All organizations have to have administrative systems and procedures in place in order to function. However, the key question is: Do the administrative systems support the main professional activities of the organization or serve as a barrier to them? Unfortunately, the development of neoliberalism as a dominant political philosophy has made 'managerialism', with its emphasis on targets and performance indicators, the norm for the most part, thereby creating a situation where extra layers of bureaucracy obstruct professionalism, rather than facilitate it (see Thompson, 2017b for further discussion of this). Being a professional means that our primary responsibilities are to our clientele and to our profession and its values. Being bureaucratic means our primary responsibility is to our employers' administrative systems – which means putting the cart before the horse. This clearly creates a tension between professionalism and bureaucracy, a point to which we shall return below.

>>> Moccasins moment <<<

Think about the professionals you may come across in your private life: teachers, nurses, doctors, solicitors and so on. If their behaviour and/or attitude were considered to be unprofessional, amateurish or bureaucratic, would you, as a user of their services, consider that acceptable?

Knowledge

I have already stressed the importance of social work's professional knowledge base. We are fortunate enough to have available to us useful insights from psychology, sociology, social policy, law and philosophy, as well as various tools and methods. As we have noted, the knowledge does not tell us what to do, but it does serve as a useful platform of understanding to help us make sense of the complex situations that are part and parcel of the world of social work practice.

Linked to this is the idea of evidence-based practice (or evidence-enriched practice as it is increasingly being called). The key idea here is that we should base our work on the best available evidence. This would include evidence from research about what has been shown to work in the past (and what has not).

 However, as with the knowledge base in general, the research will not tell us what to do, but it will give us a basis for informed practice, a platform that we can build on over time through experience and continuous professional development. This will be an important issue when we explore critically reflective practice in Section 10.

As professionals we need to not only have this knowledge base to draw upon, but also be able and willing to use it in practice (see the discussion of theorizing practice in Section 4). Sadly, I have come across a number of practitioners who seem to think that having the knowledge is enough, believing that simply having the knowledge base will somehow make them better at their job. Being able to use the appropriate knowledge in practice is what it is all about, hence the emphasis on reflective practice. For example, in my role as a consultant or expert witness I have interviewed a large number of social workers over the years and have noted that a significant proportion of them seemed to be making little or no use of the knowledge base available to them. Clearly this is not a professional approach to our practice.

We should, of course, not go to the opposite extreme and accept the knowledge base uncritically. We need to use our intelligence to question the validity and appropriateness of that knowledge base within the specific circumstances that we find ourselves in. This is why social work education is at degree level – good practice in managing the complexity involved requires critical thinking skills.

Skills

Of course, as we have already noted, critical thinking skills are not the only ones we need. Professionalism is not just about knowledge, it is also about skills – the wide range of skills we need to be effective in social work. There will be the skills that are specific to social work (or have a specific social work dimension to them, such as assessment) plus skills we share with the other helping professions (conflict management, for example) and everyday skills that we need to take to more advanced levels, such as communication. Professional skill development is therefore a matter of quality as well as quantity.

An important issue to recognize is that many so-called qualities are in fact skills. A quality is something you are assumed to either have or not, such as patience, while a skill is assumed to be something you can learn. We need to make sure that we do not make the mistake of creating barriers to our own skill development by mistaking a skill for a quality. Consider the example I gave, that of patience. If we look more closely at this, we can see that it is actually a skill, something that can be learned – that is, we can learn to become patient. Assigning patience to the category of 'quality' rather than 'skill' means that we write ourselves off unnecessarily. Patience is just one example of a skill (or set of skills) that tends to be seen as a quality.

This important point applies to ourselves (in terms of our own skill development) and to clients and carers, as helping them to develop skills that they previously felt were beyond them can be an important part of empowerment.

Values

Professionalism involves the exercise of power, and so it is important that we have a clear set of values that help to ensure that we are using such power safely, ethically and responsibly.

To sign up to a profession is to sign up to its values, to make a commitment to the principles on which it is based. Clearly, then, professional values are not an optional extra.

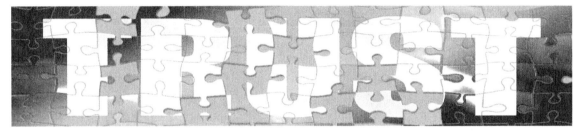

One key element of values is trust. This is linked to our earlier discussion of credibility and objective confidence. To earn that credibility we need to be trustworthy, and to earn that trust we need integrity, and integrity means acting in accordance with our values. This raises a crucial question: What does values-based practice look like in reality? That is, what is actually involved in using values in practice? There is no easy or direct answer to this, but what we should consider are the following:

- Are you aware of what your values are? Could you make them explicit if called upon to do so?

- Values are not directly visible, but how would you know that you were acting in line with your values? What would that entail?

- How would you know if your practice were not consistent with your values? What would such actions (and their consequences) look like?

There is no need for you to consider these issues alone. This can be a useful topic of discussion with colleagues – how they respond to the issues will tell you a lot about their values and about the question of values more broadly.

Accountability

The first thing to say about accountability is that it should not be confused with blame. Blame is a negative and destructive process that can so easily make a bad situation worse. It is a judgemental term. Accountability, by contrast, is a positive term. To be accountable means that you are being trusted to take responsibility for your actions, which, of course, is exactly what should be expected of a a professional.

It can be helpful to consider the root of the term 'accountability', namely *account*, a story or explanation (as in 'Can you give me an account of what happened?'). So, to be accountable means that we are able to account for our actions (or inactions), that  we can give a professional rationale for what we did or what we are planning to do. This is not about being defensive. It is, as Brechin put it some time ago, a question of *defensible* practice, rather than defensive practice (Brechin, 1993; see also Thompson, 2015a). It is certainly not about 'covering your back'. This is because when you are focusing on not getting into trouble, you are not focusing on getting the job done properly. For example, a child care social worker who is focusing on not getting their name in the newspaper is therefore not focusing on the child – and consequently is more likely to get into the trouble they are trying to avoid.

Accountable practice involves actions that we can justify by reference to our professional knowledge, skills and values. No one gets everything right, all of the time, including social workers (especially social workers, in fact, given the complexity and difficulty of the work we do). However, the key question is not whether or not we got something wrong, but whether we acted in good faith in accordance with our knowledge, skills and values.

Accountability fits very well with reflective practice. This is because, if we are practising reflectively, we should have little difficulty in giving an account of the rationale behind our practice if ever required to do so.

*** KEY POINT ***

Accountability is a positive reflection that we are being trusted as professionals. It is something to be welcomed and embraced, and should not be confused with blame or defensiveness.

Development

One clear expectation of being a professional is that we continue to get better; the longer we have been in the job, the better we should be, as we should constantly be learning and improving (hence the idea of continuous professional development, or CPD, as I mentioned earlier). The opposite of this is 'plateauing'. This refers to making initial improvements through our learning, but then reach a level where we feel comfortable and settling for that, with little or no further learning or practice development. This is often referred to as 'satisficing', an artificial amalgamation of 'satisfactory' and 'sacrificing' – in other words, settling for 'good enough', rather than trying to achieve the best results possible. This reflects a clear distinction between a bureaucratic approach (just get the job done and tick the box, good enough is good enough) and a professional one (get the job done as effectively as possible and achieve the best results, do the best we can). The latter is a values-driven approach, while the former is a defensive 'just do enough not to get into trouble' approach.

Continuous professional development means more than just attending a training course from time to time. It also involves: (i) drawing out the learning from our practice, including through supervision and team discussions (see Section 10 on reflective practice); (ii) continuing to read and undertake personal study; and (iii) making use of online resources.

An important concept in this regard is 'self-directed learning', which means taking ownership of your learning, not leaving it in the hands of others. We shall explore this important concept in more detail in Section 23. There we will examine what is involved in 'keeping the learning going' – a central part of being professional.

Identity

To have a professional identity means having a strong sense of being part of a professional community – feeling part of something bigger than ourselves, something important. Unfortunately, elitist versions of professionalism have included a focus on perks and privileges, things that set us apart from the people we serve and thereby create a hierarchy. However, as I mentioned earlier (and will re-emphasize below), professionalism does not have to be elitist and hierarchical – it can be based on partnership and empowerment.

Social work is a global enterprise. What we do is concrete and specific, wedded to the particular circumstances we are dealing with, but that is only part of the story. As we noted earlier, it is important to think holistically, to recognize the significance of the big picture. This applies just as much to the question of professionalism. There is much to be gained from having a wider sense of identity as a professional – not a member of an elitist club, but part of an important shared endeavour to make a positive difference in relation to supporting and empowering the most vulnerable members of our communities and promoting social justice.

Different countries have different organizational arrangements for supporting this sense of shared identity. In the UK the British Association of Social Workers (BASW) plays an important role in promoting the interests of social workers (and thus, indirectly, the interests of the people we serve). Internationally there is the International Federation of Social Workers (IFSW) that plays an important role in enabling groups of social workers to support one another (and our profession) across the globe.

As I have emphasized, social work is a difficult and demanding occupation. It is also one that is often misunderstood by the general public and distorted and maligned by the media. Consequently, it is essential that we support one another, individually and collectively, in responding to the major challenges involved.

Pride

Despite the common misunderstandings and misrepresentations of social work, what we do has immense significance and importance. I have often joked on training courses that undertakers are the only profession to have a 100% success rate. The serious conclusion from this is that we will not always succeed in our endeavours, despite our best efforts, and this is to be expected – just as no doctor can expect to be able to cure every patient and no police officer can expect to clear up every crime they come across. Success is always relative.

Unfortunately, though, the way the media work means that our failings (or perceived failings) are amplified and given maximum exposure, while our much more common successes pass without notice. It is unfair, of course, but that is the current state of affairs, and is likely to continue for some time yet. One sad consequence of this is that it is very easy for social workers to lose sight of: (i) how important our work is for so many people; and (ii) how much success we have overall. This will then often lead to any sense of pride being overshadowed by concerns about the unfairness of media misrepresentations and the problems this leads to (clients being unduly suspicious, for example).

The real challenge here, then, is to be able to get past the misrepresentation and reaffirm the value of the work we do. It would be great if our work could be more fully appreciated in the public sphere, but we should not allow that injustice to lead to the further injustice of our not appreciating for ourselves the crucial role of social work in making our society a humane one. The contribution we make is one to be very proud of – we should make sure that we never forget that.

Authentic professionalism

This brief overview of the key elements of professionalism should give us a clear picture of just how important professionalism is and why it is worth safeguarding and promoting. However, traditional ideas of professionalism are rooted in elitism and a sense of 'we know best'. As I argue in my *The Professional Social Worker* book, that sort of professionalism is not compatible with social work values (Thompson, 2016c). But it does not have to be that way. There is nothing inherent in the notion of professionalism that means it has to be rooted in privilege and inequality. Professionalism can – and should – be rooted in partnership and empowerment where professionals, clients and carers work together to achieve common goals. That is precisely what I mean by *authentic* professionalism – a professionalism that is true to our values.

Working in a bureaucratic organization and in a context of a lack of public appreciation of the quality and value of our work can make it very easy for us to lose sight of our professionalism. But, if we do not believe in the value of our work, we cannot expect anyone else to do so.

Professional Skills Exercise

What three skills do you see as your strongest? What can you do to make them even stronger? What three skills do you see as your least well developed? What can you do to develop them?

9. Spirituality

Spirituality is a subject that, in recent years, has been attracting a lot of attention, not only in social work, but also in the helping professions more broadly. This is a significant and welcome development, as there is a large spiritual element to social work that has long tended to be marginalized if not allowed to slip off the agenda altogether. Part of the reason for this is that traditionally there is a strong association between religion and spirituality – indeed, even a tendency to equate the two. Consequently, unless religion is explicitly part of the case scenario, there will be a tendency to neglect spiritual issues and concerns. This, as we shall see, is a costly mistake to make.

To begin with, we need to recognize that, while spirituality is a central feature of religion, religious belief is not the only form of spirituality. While not everyone is religious, everyone has spiritual needs and challenges. What we need to do, then, as far as spirituality is concerned, is to: (i) recognize the importance of religious faith in many people's lives; and (ii) take account of spiritual issues in the lives of people who have no religious faith. We shall explore each of these in turn with a view to clarifying what spirituality means for social work practice.

* * * KEY POINT * * *

Religion is not the only basis of spirituality. All people have spiritual needs and face spiritual challenges, regardless of whether they are part of a faith community.

The importance of religion

Religion is, of course, a complicated matter. There are many different religions, sharing some degree of common ground, but with many differences too. There are also, of course, huge differences in terms of how fully immersed in their religion people may be. To many members of faith communities, their religion is part of their culture and upbringing, but may have little direct bearing on their day-to-day lives, while for others, their religion may be a central feature of their lives. So, how devout a person (or family) is will vary considerably, as will the influence of their religious affiliation. In many cases this will need to be part of our assessment as it can make a big difference to the circumstances.

Religion can be seen to be significant in a number of ways, including the following:

➢ *Identity* A person's religion will often be a major feature of their identity. To fail to take account of religious aspects of a person's life may therefore, in many circumstances, amount to disrespecting that person and thereby failing to live up to our values commitment to treating people with dignity. You are  not expected to be an expert in world religions or even in your own, if you have one. However, it is valuable to have at least a basic knowledge of the key aspects of someone's religion and, most importantly, be prepared to learn more as appropriate in the circumstances. This is an important foundation of ethnically sensitive practice (tuning in to people's cultural background and its importance for them – cultural competence as it is often called). For example, in working with children and young people and wanting to incorporate an understanding of identity, culture and ethnicity, we should make sure that we do not exclude religious factors where these are relevant – and not just in general terms, but as they relate specifically to the individual and family concerned. Beware of making the mistake of seeing an individual (whether child or adult) as simply an example of a typical member of a particular faith community. It is how the person *lives their* faith that will count, and that will be different for everybody, albeit with a lot of common themes.

➢ *Support* Faith communities, as part of their religious mission, will, of course have a commitment to humanitarian endeavours and will also be committed to supporting their members as much as they reasonably can. Religion can therefore be a source of considerable social support. And, needless to say, the spiritual elements of the religion can also lead to considerable solace and inner strength, thereby proving to be very supportive. The combination of these two types of support can, in the right circumstances, prove to be highly beneficial. A failure to take account of the religious dimension of a person's life may therefore block access to significant sources of support.

➢ *Discrimination* Religious discrimination is not a new phenomenon – consider the significance of sectarianism. However, concerns about terrorism have fuelled Islamophobia on a significant scale in recent years, adding a further dimension to the issue of religious discrimination. Such problems are deeply rooted and will operate at all three levels (personal, cultural and structural) of PCS analysis, as discussed in Section 7, and so there can be no simple or straightforward answers to the challenges posed. However, this does not mean there is nothing we can do – each situation will have to be judged on its merits and responded to accordingly. One thing that is clear, though, is that failing to take account of the potential for discrimination (or, indeed, actual discrimination) is a very risky business  that could have very detrimental consequences in terms of the health and well-being of the people concerned and for the quality of our professional practice.

This is, of course, a far from comprehensive consideration of the importance of religion in social work, but it should be sufficient to establish its importance and encourage you to make sure you do not lose sight of the significance of religion.

Beyond religion

Spirituality, as I have already stressed, is not limited to religion. Whether or not we have a religious belief, we will face spiritual challenges, such as:

- How do we make sense of our life?

- How do we find (or create) a sense of purpose and direction?
- How do we know who we are and how we fit into the world?
- How do we feel part of something bigger than ourselves?

These 'existential' questions are at the heart of spirituality, as are matters of awe and wonder, wisdom, values and hope. They are relevant to us all the time, but they can be particularly to the fore and pressing at certain times – for example, when we are:

- Stressed or distressed;
- Grieving and/or traumatized;
- Ill or in chronic pain;
- Threatened or in danger;
- Facing major change;
- In conflict or facing hostility;
- Under the influence of alcohol or drugs; and/or
- Experiencing mental health problems

In other words, they can be to the fore precisely in those circumstances where social work intervention is likely to be needed.

Religion can be one way of addressing our spiritual needs and challenges. However, we need to remember that: (i) a significant proportion of non-religious people are generally able to address these spiritual issues with at least some degree of success, so religion is not the only potentially successful spiritual path to follow; and (ii) it is not always the case that religious people will have their spiritual needs met through their religion – at times of adversity, religious faith can be strengthened, but the opposite can also occur in that faith can be questioned or even abandoned (see, for example, Holloway, 2004).

Spirituality raises a number of important issues for people, especially when they are facing adversity, are feeling vulnerable or going through significant change. A social work practice that failed to take spirituality into consideration would therefore be missing out on so many significant factors and could easily be standing in the way of progress, rather than playing an active part in facilitating it.

It is therefore important that we do not restrict our view of spirituality by seeing it simply as a dimension of religion and thereby fall foul of the pitfall of assuming that, where religion is not of major concern, neither is spirituality. Spirituality is about being *human*, as indeed is social work.

 Spirituality is an ever-present feature of human life, but its significance looms large when people are suffering or struggling in some respect(s). It is therefore essential that we do not lose sight of the spiritual dimensions of our work.

The implications for practice

As with social work in general, what we do in relation to spirituality can either help or hinder. Our actions can play a part in helping people achieve spiritual fulfilment (that is, help them meet their spiritual needs and rise to their spiritual challenges) or contribute to spiritual diminishment (making it hard for them to address their spiritual needs and challenges). So, one clear implication for practice is that we need to make sure that we do not lose sight of the spiritual dimension of people's lives and, indeed, of our work itself – another reason why reflective practice needs to be a central feature of how we tackle our work.

Holloway and Moss (2012) talk about the idea of accompanying people on their spiritual journey, of being a 'fellow traveller'. This fits well with the well-established idea in social work that the most valuable resource at our disposal is our self (our human presence – see the discussion of 'human connection' in Section 13). What has run counter to this in recent years is the 'consumerist' approach I mentioned earlier and to which we will return later, with its emphasis on providing or commissioning services – a set of primarily (pseudo-)commercial transactions pushing the human connection to the margins (or out of the picture altogether).

The fellow traveller analogy is a good general principle. To this we can add the following specific points:

➢ *Assessment* In gathering information about the situation to form a picture in any case we are dealing with, we should not limit ourselves to the practical matters, but also consider the spiritual dimensions – for example, what part  meaning, purpose and direction are playing in this situation. A key part of this will be *empathy* – trying to see the situation from the point of view of the person(s) we are trying to help and thereby trying to get a sense of where they are coming from spiritually.

➢ *Intervention* Likewise, in trying to address the needs and problems identified in the assessment and to capitalize on the strengths and resilience factors, we should not lose sight of where the person(s) concerned are up to in their lives in terms of the key elements of spirituality highlighted above.

➢ *Discrimination* The oppressive consequences of being discriminated against consistently and persistently are likely to include a considerable spiritual diminishment. We should therefore recognize that a commitment to anti-discriminatory practice is not only a legal and ethical requirement, but also a spiritual matter.

➢ *Mental health* There is now a growing literature on the significance of spirituality in the mental health field. It is increasingly being recognized that the challenges people with mental health problems face are in large part rooted in spirituality. My own experience as a mental health social worker reinforces this. When it comes to emotion-related problems, such as anxiety and depression, drawing links with spirituality (meaning, purpose, direction, identity, connection, hope) is a very easy thing to do and a very fruitful one. The growing critique of the medical model of mental health encourages us to look at mental health more holistically, and this includes taking account of spiritual matters. Issues associated with psychosis are perhaps not so obviously linked with spirituality, but there is still much value in applying our growing awareness of spiritual issues to the full range of mental health concerns.

> *Child care* A central part of growing up is developing a sense of identity and understanding how we fit into the world. This also involves developing a sense of purpose and direction and finding or creating meaning. The growing child also develops a sense of connectedness to other people and their culture, and potentially to wider aspects of the world (a community, a nation, a religion or whatever). He or she develops hopes and aspirations, learns values and explores the world with a sense of awe and wonder. Clearly these are spiritual matters, even though, as we shall see in Section 11, child development is often described in much more technical terms that can lead us to lose sight of the spiritual issues involved. Where children are neglected, abused, abandoned or otherwise led into distressing circumstances, there will be many spiritual needs and challenges that emerge from such situations. Trying to work with children and young people in such circumstances without taking account of spiritual factors is likely to hamper us significantly in terms of offering appropriate care, support and protection and may actually mean that our efforts to help are counterproductive doing more harm than good.

> *Ageing* There are various challenges involved in growing old and ultimately facing death, especially in an ageist society that devalues older people. For example, in Sue Thompson's important work on reciprocity (S. Thompson, 2013; 2015) she points out that, in our younger lives being able to give as well as receive, to contribute and feel useful are important aspects of not only our self-esteem, but also our spiritual fulfilment. However, the way care services

work will often result in opportunities for reciprocity to be reduced, if not removed altogether, as characterized by the common attitude of: 'It's OK, I'll do that for you', with little or no opportunity to give in return. The detrimental impact of this denial of reciprocity cannot be over-emphasized. Coping with it is just one of the many existential or spiritual challenges that people are likely to face in later life.

➢ *Loss and grief* We shall examine issues of loss and grief in more detail in Section 21, but for now I want to make the point that experiencing a major loss is a highly spiritual event, as it can undermine our sense of security and stability, even our sense of self ('biographical disruption' as it is known in technical terms). Our world gets turned upside down and our framework of meaning is challenged. Things do not get much more spiritual than that! What makes this particularly significant is that, in social work, loss and grief issues are never far away (Thompson, 2012b; Thompson and Thompson, 2016).

>>> Moccasins moment <<<

Imagine being in a situation where people are kind enough to look after you, but you have no opportunity to do anything in return, no opportunity to give, contribute or be useful. What impact do you think that would have on your self-esteem and your spiritual well-being?

There is, of course, much more that could be said about the practice implications of spirituality for social work, so your attention is directed to the *Guide to further learning* at the end of the manual. It is certainly a subject worthy of further investigation and study, and one that can make a hugely positive difference to the quality and effectiveness of our work and, importantly, our job satisfaction and, linked to that, our own spiritual needs.

Unfortunately, many people who engage with issues of spirituality seem to regard this as an opportunity to engage in highly flowery language and abandon any sense of rationality, as if entering the realm of spirituality can be interpreted to mean 'anything goes'. This is a great pity, as spirituality is a serious matter relating to the existential challenges we all face in life, and it is particularly relevant at the times when people are struggling or suffering and in need of help and support.

Spirituality Exercise

How would you characterize your own spirituality if you were asked to describe it? What would you see as the main ways in which you achieve a sense of purpose and direction? What gives your life meaning? And, importantly, how might an awareness of your own spirituality help you tune in to other people's spiritual issues?

10. Reflective practice

I have already made several references to the importance of reflective practice, so it should come as no surprise to learn that I consider the issues we are going to be exploring in this section to be fundamental to good practice. Reflective practice is not an optional extra, and, as we shall see, it is certainly not a luxury we cannot afford.

What is reflective practice?

I have often been asked on training courses I have run about reflective practice how I would characterize reflective practice in one sentence, and my reply would always be the same: 'You've got a brain, use it'. A fuller definition would be:

> Reflective practice is intelligent, thoughtful practice informed by professional knowledge, skills and values.

One helpful way of understanding reflective practice is to consider what non-reflective practice amounts to, namely basing our actions on habit, routine, guesswork or just copying others.

Much of what we do in life is based on an unthinking, more or less automatic response to situations. That will get us by in very many situations, but it is certainly not enough for what we will face in social work practice. Reflective practice can therefore be understood as practice in which:

➢ We use our intelligence: we think things through carefully *before* we engage in practice (reflection-for-action) – for example, planning before an interview or a meeting; *while* we are engaged in practice (reflection-in-action) – thinking on our feet; and *after* we have been engaged in practice with one or more people (reflection-on-action) – reviewing what has happened to make sense of it and to draw out the lessons that we can learn from.

- We draw on our professional knowledge base by theorizing practice, as discussed earlier – that is, we make sense of the circumstances we are involved in by making use of our study of human life through psychology, sociology and so on. In this way, we make sure that our practice is *informed* practice – intelligent, thoughtful practice. As I explained earlier, our professional knowledge base will not provide us with direct answers, but it will give us a foundation of understanding on which to build.

- We use our social work skills and seek to develop those skills, to take them to a more advanced level so that we can be as effective as possible, leaving as little to chance as we can. The knowledge base is of relatively little value if we do not have the skills to capitalize on the insights it offers us.

- We underpin our practice with values – that is, we act with integrity. Knowledge is of little use if we do not have the skills to benefit from it. But skills are potentially quite dangerous if not used within an ethical framework of values and integrity.

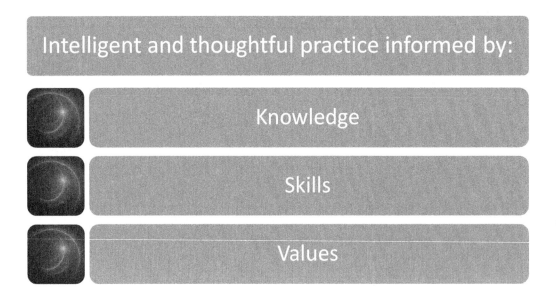

Intelligent and thoughtful practice informed by:

Knowledge

Skills

Values

Unfortunately, the use by universities and colleges of a reflective log or diary as a means of promoting and assessing learning has led a lot of people to assume that reflective practice is nothing but keeping a log or diary. In reality, this type of activity is just one small part of reflective practice.

What is just as unfortunate if not more so is that this distortion of what reflective practice is all about so often leads to another distortion, namely the frequently aired view that: 'I don't have time to do reflective practice'. It is as if reflective practice is a luxury they cannot afford, rather than a fundamental element of good practice. What is presumably meant is: 'I do not have time to keep a reflective diary', which is a reasonable enough comment (although not altogether beyond challenge in terms of time and workload management skills). However, to assume that busy professionals do not have time for reflective practice at all is highly dangerous. It is the equivalent of saying:

- I do not have time to think or use my intelligence.
- I do not have time to use my professional knowledge base.
- I do not have time to use or develop my social work skills.
- I do not have time to practise with integrity.
- I do not have time to be a professional.
- I am prepared to respond to complex situations that can have an important bearing on vulnerable people's lives in an unthinking, uncritical way, based on habit, guesswork and copying others.

In reality, the truth of reflective practice is: the busier or more pressurized we are, the more reflective we need to be; the more we need to focus, to think, plan, learn, develop our skills, use our knowledge, be guided by our values and make the best use of the limited time and resources available to us. Saying 'I haven't got time for reflective practice' and then pressing on regardless without clarity about what we are doing and what we are dealing with is probably one of the most dangerous things we can do in social work.

What is critical practice?

One of the hallmarks of reflective practice is self-awareness, being able to tune in to what is going on around us, what effect we are having on the situation and what effect the situation is having on us. What we also need to complement this, returning to our earlier discussion of the need for holistic thinking, is some degree of *social awareness*. That is, we need to be tuned in to how wider social factors like poverty, deprivation, discrimination and oppression can play a highly significant role in shaping people's problems. Atomistic practice that pays no attention to wider social issues will be missing out on some highly significant aspects of the situation, thereby settling for a very limited understanding of what they are dealing with. There is therefore considerable potential for doing more harm than good by unwittingly reinforcing discrimination, for example.

Critical practice is therefore practice that is aware of such wider issues, takes them into consideration in terms of assessment and demonstrates a commitment to challenging the destructive processes involved where possible. Also often referred to as progressive or emancipatory practice, it is an approach that is sensitive to wider sociopolitical factors and therefore draws on sociological insights as well as psychological ones.

What is critically reflective practice?

It is quite possible to have reflective practice that is not critical – for example, an approach to practice that draws on psychological insights, but takes no account of the equally important sociological understandings that social workers also need in order to do justice to the complexities involved.

Similarly, it is quite possible for practice to be critical without being reflective. For example, consider the discussion of 'dogmatic reductionism' in Section 7 where I highlighted the dangers of a rigid and simplistic approach to discrimination and oppression. There is a certain irony that some people who describe their work as 'critical' are happy to accept uncritically certain ideas and approaches. Thankfully, such people are in a minority.

It does not follow, then, that critical practice will be reflective or reflective practice will be critical. What, then, is involved in critically reflective practice? Thompson and Thompson (2018) break it down into critical breadth and critical depth:

- *Critical breadth* This entails going beyond the immediate circumstances and looking more holistically at the situation, taking account, for example, of the significance of issues such as poverty and deprivation; discrimination and oppression; and other social processes, institutions and structures. In other words, it is a matter of avoiding atomism.

- *Critical depth* This involves not taking situations at face value, being prepared to look beneath the surface and look for underlying processes and influences. When, for example, we criticize someone for accepting something 'uncritically', what we are saying is that it would have been wiser to look beneath the surface and not just accept what initially seems to be the case.

Both critical breadth and critical depth reinforce the idea that well-developed analytical skills are an important part of the effective social worker's repertoire.

Why do we need critically reflective practice?

First, let's consider why we need reflective practice. If we return to our discussion earlier of 'I don't have time to do reflective practice', we should be able to see what risks we are taking if we fail to engage with reflective practice. We will, in effect, be relying on habit, routine, guesswork and/or just copying others – hardly a basis for professional practice.

Consider, for example, how dangerous our decision making would be if we were not using our intelligence, not drawing on our professional knowledge base, our skills and values – especially our values.

Without reflective practice there would also be less scope for learning, creativity and job satisfaction and therefore greater scope for dissatisfaction, burnout and stress.

And, if it is not *critically* reflective practice, we can lose out on:

➤ Recognizing the *social* nature of the circumstances we encounter in our work and the need for a sociological understanding (Thompson, 2018). This takes us back to our earlier discussion of the importance of a holistic approach, one that sees the big picture, so that the significance of wider factors will not be missed. Without that big picture outlook, there is a danger that we are seeing a distorted picture that places undue emphasis on the individual or personal factors at the expensive of the cultural and structural factors that also have a part to play.

>>> Moccasins moment <<<

How are you likely to feel if ever you encounter a situation where you, your family or someone you care about were to receive help from a social worker on autopilot, someone who is not using their knowledge, skills and values and is not thinking through the issues they are dealing with?

➤ Without a critical perspective we may miss not only wider social factors, such as poverty and deprivation, discrimination and oppression (critical breadth), but also deeper issues that are not immediately apparent without some degree of critical analysis (to recognize underlying conflicts, abusive dynamics and so on – critical depth). One of the points that was hammered home quite firmly as part of my own social work training was the need to look beneath the surface of the 'presenting' problem and explore the significance of the 'underlying' problem(s) – for example, not taking problematic behaviour on a child's part at face value as 'emotional disturbance' (which is how it may be presented in a referral), but, rather, looking more deeply into what could well be better explained by underlying family dynamics (as family therapy teaches us – Taibbi, 2018).

➢ There is a danger that, if we are not approaching our work in a critically reflective way, we will not be tuned in to the complexities involved and may actually do more harm than good (imagine, for example, a white social worker working with a black family and taking no cognizance of racism and thereby walking over the family's feelings due to a failure to consider the sensitive issues involved).

The price we (plus the people we serve and our very profession) pay for not ensuring that our work is rooted in critically reflective practice is therefore a very high one.

Beware of the common myths and misunderstandings around reflective practice – for example, the idea that it is a luxury we cannot afford (because we are too busy) or that it is simply a matter of keeping a reflective log or diary.

11. Growth and change

In this section we look at why it is important to have a good understanding of human development. This is because, while each person we come across seems to be just as they are, in reality, they – and we – are in the process of changing. To put it technically, each of us is on a journey through life, constantly changing and adapting to our environment. Just as the Earth appears to be still when in reality it is moving through space at quite a speed, we are constantly in a state of 'becoming'. Having some idea of where people are up to in their lives and where they are heading can often be of value in developing a helpful assessment. This should become clearer in the pages that follow as we examine the significance of human growth and development.

Ages and stages

This subject matter is traditionally discussed in terms of 'ages and stages'. This can be helpful, provided that we do not become too rigid in our understanding of what we mean by 'stages'. We all develop in unique ways as time passes, but there are broad shared patterns that can be discerned, common themes that can give us useful information. When I was a social work student what was emphasized in this regard was the idea of the 'broad spectrum of the norm' – that is, the need to recognize that what counts as 'normal' can be quite diverse; we should not think too narrowly about what is 'normal development'.

What experience has taught me since then is that we need to be clear about what we mean by the 'norm' or 'normal' and not use these terms in a judgemental sense. The idea is not to tell people how they 'should' develop, but to be aware that there *may* be problems indicated by a person's development not following the *usual* patterns.

In that last paragraph I highlighted two words, 'may' and 'usual'. This is because, in terms of 'may', we need to recognize that someone developing in a different way from most other people is not necessarily a problem. This is a mistake that was quite common in the past in relation to sexual development when a preference for same-sex relationships was perceived to be an aberration, a sign of illness or pathology – not being in the majority was seen as a problem (rather than prejudice and discrimination about sexual diversity being seen as a problem). However, there can be times when development not following the usual path is indeed a sign of a problem – for example, when a young child is 'failing to thrive' because they are not receiving enough nutrition as a result of neglect. So, we have to keep this 'may' in mind.

As far as 'usual' is concerned, we need to bear in mind that it is in this sense that we are using the term 'normal' – that is, the norm is the statistical majority and refers to what generally happens (as opposed to the sense of the norm as what *should* happen, what would be considered 'wrong' or worrisome if it did not happen – for example, if a boy were to like playing with dolls).

❊ ❊ ❊ KEY POINT ❊ ❊ ❊

We do not want to be judgemental, but nor should we risk missing significant indicators that something is wrong or in need of attention.

It is important to acknowledge that, sadly, the whole idea of human growth and development is characterized by common stereotypes and judgemental expectations (about what *should* happen). As values-driven social workers, we need to be very aware of this, but also need to make sure that we do not allow developmental problems or issues to be missed. For example, as we shall note below, adolescent behaviour can be challenging at times, but it is important that we are able to distinguish between 'normal' adolescent behaviour (that is not necessarily anything to be concerned about) and behaviour that may be indicative of abuse or other legitimate concerns (a high level of family tension, for example).

In considering human growth and development we need to bear in mind that there are different 'strands' to development. Traditionally the focus has been on the biological strand (with frequent references to 'the organism', rather than 'the person' – a very telling use of terminology). So, in addition to biological development (or 'maturation' to use the technical term), we also have to consider:

- *Psychological development* This will include cognitive, emotional and behavioural (and the interactions across the three).

- *Moral development* Learning about cultural expectations and developing a sense of right and wrong.

- *Social development* Becoming, and remaining a functioning member of society, with all that this implies. Whatever society we live in will have complex rules, processes and institutions, each of which can have a profound effect on us and our development.

- *Existential development* Also sometimes referred to as spiritual or ontological development, this refers to our development and maintenance of a sense of identity, purpose and direction.

We therefore need to be careful to make sure that we do not fall into the trap of assuming that 'human growth and development' is exclusively or even mainly biological – it is one dimension among the many that make us such complex creatures as human beings.

Child development

In terms of stages, childhood begins with pregnancy, birth and infancy, of course. From these times right through childhood and on to adolescence, the child will be vulnerable in various ways and thus in need of protection. Working with children will therefore always need to contain an element of protection.

The child will also be impressionable, in the sense that they will constantly be learning. One important consideration, therefore, will be: What is the child learning? Is such learning helpful or harmful? In what circumstances might we need to intervene to try and influence what a child is learning? For example, are they learning how to hurt and harm (because they are being hurt or harmed) or are they learning to cooperate, to help and to nurture (because they are receiving cooperation, help and nurture)?

As social workers we are not expected to be experts in child development, but we do need to:

- Have at least a good basic understanding of the issues involved;
- Be prepared to keep learning – for example, by looking things up when we are not sure;
- Work closely with relevant colleagues (health visitors, GPs and so on) as appropriate; and
- Constantly be tuned in to the significance of child development and its various strands.

Adolescent development

Adolescence is that time of transition between childhood and adulthood. It is a time characterized by various stereotypes and misunderstandings – for example, the idea that adolescents are necessarily rebellious (in reality, most are not, although some degree of exploration and testing of boundaries is very common indeed).

Adolescence, because of the significant upheavals involved, can be a difficult time, for the adolescents themselves and for the people who live or work with them. There are no easy answers or formula solutions when it comes to working with adolescents, particularly adolescents who are having problems of some sort. However, it can be helpful to bear in mind the following pointers:

➤ A major challenge for adolescents is managing the tension between the comfort zone of what they are used to in terms of a child's behaviour, thinking patterns and emotional responses on the one hand, and the pressures (internal and external) to adopt more adult patterns, on the other. This can result in inconsistent responses (childlike one minute, much more mature the next). Consequently, we can be helpful by being aware of this tension and being appropriately supportive – for example, accepting the childlike behaviours (but maintaining appropriate boundaries of behaviour – see below) without making the young person concerned feel guilty about not yet being fully adult, while recognizing and affirming the adult behaviours.

➤ There will be loss issues involved. However appealing adulthood may appear, there will be certain comforts, pleasures and reassurances that childhood offers (not just in adolescence, but throughout our lives). Letting go of certain elements of childhood can therefore evoke a grief reaction. As we shall see in section 21, grief is a reaction to any significant loss, and not just to death. We therefore need to be sensitive to the grief issues and respond in appropriate ways.

➤ Adolescence can begin in the pre-teen years and last well into our twenties. Consequently, it is not a simple process of transition, but, rather, a set of very many transitions over a period of years. Because of this, adolescents, like children, will go through many changes and their needs will also change in some ways at the various points throughout this lengthy process. We therefore have to 'tune in' to where each individual is up to in their own developmental process and assess carefully what the issues are, rather than rely on a simplistic generalized view of adolescence. For example, aspects of adolescence will be different in significant ways for gay teenagers, for young people with disabilities and for young carers who may be forced into an adult role early. It is not a matter of one size fits all.

➤ Because of the changes and insecurities involved in adolescence, young people can respond positively to clear boundaries, provided that these are managed tactfully and sensitively and not seen as unnecessary restrictions.

Working with adolescents can be challenging work, but it can also be very rewarding and worthwhile.

Adult transitions

For a long time the major focus in human growth and development was on childhood and adolescence, as if we stop growing and developing once we reach adulthood. The reality, of course, is that we continue to change and develop throughout our lives (including in old age – see below). We are constantly encountering new challenges and therefore being faced with opportunities to learn and grow.

With this in mind we need to make sure that we recognize the various transitions that are likely to be part of adulthood for most, but not necessarily all, including:

- Entering the world of work;
- Establishing independence;
- Marriage or equivalent long-term relationship;
- Becoming a parent;
- Children leaving home; and
- Retirement.

As with adolescents, there will be loss issues involved in each transition, and so we find ourselves once again in the territory to be discussed in more detail in Section 21, that of loss and grief.

We should therefore be careful to avoid the mistake of assuming that being an adult is somehow static, a fixed status, rather than an ongoing process that involves a series of highly significant transitions. Being clear where someone is up to in their life course journey will often give us much useful information for our assessment and the work we subsequently do based on that assessment.

Growing old

Old age is, of course, a continuation of adulthood, and not separate from it. We need to be very wary of the very common, well-established ageist assumption that older people are a separate group from the rest of society. This tendency towards marginalization and exclusion is very harmful and creates an unhelpful distorted understandings of the reality of old age. So, step one towards good practice in this area must be the abandonment of any such stereotypes and assumptions – that is, we need to 'unlearn' what our ageist society teaches us about older people.

As we reach the later stages of life, we can face changes in some of the other developmental strands:

- *Biological* Health problems and other related challenges can increase in old age, but we must beware of making the assumption that ageing itself is some sort of disease process.

- *Psychological* There can be significant psychological challenges for us as we grow older, but it is essential that we do not: (i) assume that these are inevitable as a 'natural' part of ageing; or (ii) overemphasize their significance. As in all things, a balanced assessment is needed.

- *Social* The prevalence of ageism means that there are significant social issues that arise (mainly social barriers) for people when they reach old age. These can have a significant impact on the other developmental strands.

*** KEY POINT ***

Damaging ageist assumptions and stereotypes are firmly embedded in culture, and therefore part of most people's upbringing. If we are not careful, we can find them influencing us without our knowing. An anti-ageist approach is therefore essential.

- *Existential* Later life involves a number of existential challenges, partly as a result of social factors as mentioned, and partly as a result of our mortality and the need to face death (see below). Old age can also be a time of significant loss – for example, as close contemporaries (those we knew personally plus those we did not – actors, musicians, public figures and so on).

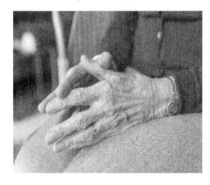

One particularly significant aspect of ageism is that it propagates the view that development ends when we reach old age. Older people are people first and foremost and therefore on their own journey of development, like everybody else.

Facing death

The notion that we live in a 'death-denying' society is a long-standing one. Perhaps denial of death is not the right term, as we all know that we are going to die one day. It is more a case of generally not being prepared to face up to death, to think through the implications of being mortal and therefore having a finite lifespan. This can lead to situations where people find having to face up to death even more difficult than it needs to be, even more of a challenge.

There is little we can do about this (beyond death education programmes), but what we can do is to learn to face our own mortality so that, whenever we are supporting others in facing death (when a death occurs or when a terminal illness is diagnosed, for example), we are better placed to do so, because we will not be struggling with our own fears and anxieties (or at least less so).

The *Guide to further learning* at the end of the manual lists some useful literature that can be very helpful in this regard.

Identity and its importance

Underpinning the various ages and stages is our sense of identity, the linking thread that holds it all together. Whatever point in the life course the people we are working with are at, we need to be sensitive to how they perceive their situation, what it means to them in terms of their sense of who they are. This is because this is what will be influencing their thoughts, feelings and actions.

Identity is also vitally important because so many of the problems and challenges we encounter in social work are linked in some way to identity. Consider the following examples:

- Traumatic experiences can leave us feeling unsure of who we are (see Section 21);

- Aggression and violence will often be a response to being humiliated and thereby having self-esteem and self-respect attacked;

- The problematic use of alcohol and other drugs can be linked with problems relating to identity and not feeling comfortable with who we are;

- Mental health problems, whether neurotic (anxiety and depression) or psychotic (schizophrenic conditions, for example), can also be closely linked to identity issues; and

- Our value commitment to dignity is also very much about identity and self-respect.

Wherever we go and whatever we do in social work, we should never lose sight of the central role of identity – it is a focal point of each person's life. It is therefore essential to make sure that we do not lose sight of identity issues, including our own.

Human Development Exercise

Where would you see yourself in terms of your life course? What are the important issues that you face in your life at this particular point? To what extent are these issues typical of your location along the life course spectrum of development and to what extent are they specific to you? How might a knowledge of your own developmental issues help you to support others with their challenges?

12. Health and well-being

There is a two-way relationship between social work and health. On the one hand, stress can have an adverse effect on health, and so the work we do as social workers that helps people reduce their stress levels can have a positive effect on their health. On the other hand, health problems will often be a key factor in the circumstances that lead to the need for social work involvement, especially mental health issues. In this section we therefore explore some of the practice implications of the complex inter-relationships between social work and health.

Defining health and well-being

Although these two terms are widely used, each of them is difficult to define specifically. This is partly because they are used in slightly different ways at different times or by different people. For example, the World Health Organization defines health as: 'a state of complete physical, mental and social well-being and not merely the absence of disease or infirmity' (http://www.who.int/suggestions/faq/en/). However, this can be seen as an 'aspirational' definition, in the sense that it is a value statement about what our approach to health issues *should* be like; it is not necessarily a reflection of how issues of health are actually addressed in practice for the most part. It could also be argued that this broad definition incorporates well-being into health, when in reality health and well-being are two separate (but related) matters. It is possible to be in good health, but have a low level of well-being (for example, if you are grieving or otherwise distressed), and it is also possible to be in poor health, but still have a high level of well-being.

So, for present purposes, I will be using health to refer to the absence of illness, injury or infirmity and well-being as quality of life. The two are closely connected, but, as we shall later, it is important to recognize that there are significant differences also.

Social aspects of health and well-being

The healthcare world understandably has a strong biological emphasis. Unfortunately, though, this can often lead to a neglect of the other dimensions (psychological, social and existential/spiritual). This is often where social work comes in, to address these other elements of health, especially the social ones. All of the following social factors can be very significant in relation to health and, of course, well-being:

- *Poverty* Struggling to cope on a limited income can not only bring health-affecting stress, but also other factors, such as poor diet, smoking and alcohol consumption. It goes without saying that poverty will also have an adverse effect on well-being much of the time.

- *Housing and homelessness* Closely linked to poverty, poor-quality housing (damp or overcrowded, for example) can lead to a number of health problems, and homelessness will do so even more so, of course. Once again, the detrimental impact on well-being is fairly self-evident.

- *Employment* Stressful, hazardous or insecure employment can make a huge negative difference to health and well-being, and unemployment will likewise be a significant source of pressures and problems for many people.

- *Discrimination* The oppressive consequences of discrimination can affect both physical and mental health and, of course, discrimination within the health system can also be a negative factor.

- *Conflict and tensions* All of the above can create health-affecting conflicts and tensions, as can many of the other issues we encounter in social work. There can be a vicious circle whereby conflicts and tensions affect well-being; well-being affects health; poor health creates additional conflicts and tensions; and so on.

A key part of our role as social workers in relation to health issues is therefore to address, wherever possible, the social aspects, partly with a view to improving health and partly to address the social problems that are contributing to poor health.

Health and disability

The traditional approach to disability is one that frames physical and/or mental impairments in a medical model. However, this approach has long been heavily criticized for its oppressive consequences. The development of the 'social model' of disability has been significant, and it is now widely adopted.

*** KEY POINT ***

Health issues have a very strong *personal* impact, but we should not allow this to lead us to neglect the *cultural* and *structural* aspects that are also very important.

The basic premise of the social model of disability is that it is the way society is organized and social attitudes that disable people with impairments, rather than the impairments themselves having a disabling effect. For example, it is not the fact that someone cannot walk or climb stairs that prevents them from participating fully in social life, it is the absence of ramps and lifts and prejudicial attitudes that are based on a range of false assumptions (for example, that people with disabilities are somehow less intelligent). In a nutshell, the medical model is disempowering as it focuses on what disabled people cannot do, whereas the social model is empowering because it focuses on removing social and attitudinal barriers.

One of the major implications of this for social work is that, while there will often be a need to provide or commission care services for people with disabilities, we need to see this role within a context of empowerment and rights, not of illness and inability. These are important issues, and so it is important that you make sure that you are au fait with the social model of disability and its implications – see the *Guide to further learning* at the end of the manual.

The social work role in relation to health

It is not at all contentious to say that everything we do in social work is geared, directly or indirectly, towards promoting well-being. But what of health? Where does that fit into the picture?

To answer this we need to come back to the two-way relationship I mentioned: health issues and social work issues intertwine and influence one another.

There can be settings where health issues are to the fore (for social workers based in hospitals or with GP surgeries, for example) and the major focus is on addressing personal and social challenges that are affecting health (on the understanding that improved health will play a stronger part in tackling the personal and social issues involved). However, in all settings, not just those with a specific focus on healthcare, health issues can play a significant part in the circumstances that the social worker has been called upon to deal with. For example, there may be health issues that are affecting an older person's ability to cope alone in the community and avoid residential care – an improvement in health could perhaps avoid the need to give up their home. Similarly, child care problems arising from a parent's health problem may be alleviated by addressing the health care issues.

From a practice point of view, what we need to recognize is that, because health and well-being issues are closely inter-related, we need to include health issues in our thinking and thus in or assessment work. Further, because of this, we need to be able to work effectively with health colleagues and thereby take seriously the challenges of working in partnership (as discussed in Section 6).

 Beware of making the mistake of assuming that health is a matter solely for health professionals. It is an important factor in so much of what we do in social work.

Mental health and well-being

The notion of 'mental illness' is a highly contested one. There is a long history of scholars and professionals criticizing the dominant psychiatric view of mental health problems as 'symptoms' of an illness. It is no coincidence that former patients often refer to themselves as 'survivors'. We therefore need to be aware that the current mental health system is far from unproblematic.

As we have seen, all health problems have social, psychological and spiritual dimensions, mental health especially so. However, the dominant thinking in psychiatry is mainly biomedical in its focus. There is therefore an important role for social workers to provide a counterbalance by: (i) taking into account the problems associated with a biomedical model (stigma and discrimination, for example); and (ii) trying to make sure that the psychological, social and spiritual aspects are also being addressed as appropriate.

There are no simple, straightforward ways of doing this, but some basic social work principles will stand us in good stead:

- *Assessment* We need to make sure that we carry out a thorough assessment and do not rely on medical labels or psychiatric diagnoses that can be misleading and which, besides, never tell the whole story.

- *Holistic thinking* We need to see the big picture and make sure we take account of the wider social factors as well as the psychological and spiritual issues, despite the common major focus in mental health circles on the biomedical.

- *Critically reflective practice* Mental health and well-being is a complex field which, despite the claims to scientific standing of the psychiatric establishment, we still know relatively little about. We therefore need to think very carefully about what we are doing, draw on the knowledge we do have available and look beneath the surface of a simplistic biomedical model that does not do justice to the complexities involved.

- *Partnership working* Although we will find ourselves working with people who adopt a psychiatric model that is at odds with social work values and perspectives, we none the less need to have the skills and commitment to work effectively in partnership.

Conclusion

Health is a complex matter in many ways, especially in the highly contested area of mental health. This presents a number of challenges for social workers, but it is essential that we manage to rise to them and support one another in doing so. We are not health professionals, but it would be a major mistake not to recognize that health issues are often very important aspects of what we do.

As we have noted, health will affect well-being and well-being will affect health. This can be in a positive or a negative sense. A key part of our role is to try to make sure, as far as possible, that the relationship between health and well-being is a positive one in both directions.

Health and Well-being Exercise

Think about the different 'branches' of social work (child care, working with adults, youth justice, mental health and so on). Think about the potential ways health could be a key factor in some aspects of each of these. What implications might these issues have for your own field of work (or the field of work you plan on working in?

13. Human connection

One of the themes that was strongly emphasized when I undertook my professional social work training was the idea that social work is basically human to human connection – we must never lose sight of the fact that the people we are serving are human beings (with all that this entails), nor too must we lose sight of the fact that we are human too (with all that that entails). In this section, therefore, we look in more detail at what that means in practice.

Authentic connection

Martin Buber was a theologian who introduced a distinction that has been widely used in various professions where authentic connection with people is a key part of the job, and that includes social work, of course. He distinguished between I-Thou and I-it interactions (Buber, 2004). These can be understood as follows:

> ➤ *I-Thou* This refers to what happens when each party shows respect and concern towards the other. It is when we form a genuine human connection, really listening to each other and being concerned to make the interaction a positive and enriching one for us both. This can range from a very profound and meaningful interaction (for example, in supporting someone who is grieving and wants to talk about their profound and intense feelings of loss) to a straightforward, fairly superficial encounter in buying something in a shop. It is not the purpose or significance of the interaction that counts, but, rather, how it is conducted – how each party relates to the other.

> ➤ *I-it* This type of interaction is where one person treats the other in a purely instrumental way. That is, it is purely a matter of 'getting the job done' or achieving whatever it is you want from the interaction. It is one sided and

focuses just on your own interests. You may get what you want from the interaction, but neither party will be enriched by it.

Consider the following two very similar (but also very different) scenarios:

- You go into a shop, pick up the item you want from the shelf and go up to the cashpoint. The sales assistant smiles and greets you as you arrive. They make eye contact as they give you your change and thanks you for your custom. You leave the shop feeling positive about having had good service. The sales assistant feels good about having provided good service and this makes their working life more pleasant. It has been a win-win encounter.

- You go into a shop, pick up the item you want from the shelf and go up to the cashpoint. The sales assistant is chatting to their colleague. They make no eye contact with you and carry on chatting. They take your item from the counter, scan it and announce the price to you. You offer them the money, which they take, but still no eye contact and no verbal contact other than telling you what the price is. They put your change on the counter and carry on chatting to their colleague. You leave the shop with your purchase and your change. The transaction has therefore been successful. However, the chances are that you will feel less than satisfied and possibly quite annoyed. The sales assistant will not have benefited from the encounter either. It is a lose-lose situation, even though you both 'got the job done'.

This example is a relatively straightforward retail transaction. Just imagine how damaging an I-it approach could be in a social work context where we are working with people who are distressed, anxious, afraid, grieving, traumatized and/or desperate. And that damage will be not only to the people we serve, but also to our own reputation and that of our profession.

Buber made the crucial point that I-Thou interactions *humanize* both parties, while I-it interactions *dehumanize* both parties. This is, of course, a matter of dignity, as we discussed earlier. As social workers, we should never lose sight of this

For some people, I-it interactions are the norm because they lack the social skills to do any better than that and they are oblivious to the problems such interactions cause. However, anyone can engage in I-it interactions when they are tired, in a hurry, distracted or otherwise not at their best. This includes social workers. For example, I have come across situations where the social worker carried out an assessment by simply reading out questions from a form and writing in the answers, with no warmth or human connection. Technically, it got the job done, but, professionally, it was far from adequate.

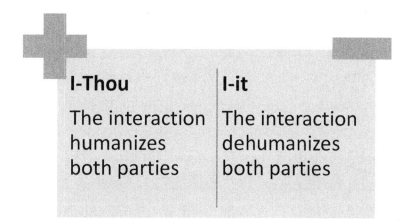

I-Thou	I-it
The interaction humanizes both parties	The interaction dehumanizes both parties

It should be clear, then, that what we need in social work is authentic human connection, I-Thou, not I-it. We need the self-awareness that is part of reflective practice to ensure that we are consistent in doing this and do not allow habit, routine, low morale or pressure of work to push us into working at an I-it level.

Listening

There is a significant danger with the idea of listening. It is one of the most important parts of social work practice, and yet so many people pay it relatively little attention because they think it is an obvious point and not worthy of further consideration. 'Of course, it's important to listen, it goes without saying', commented one participant on a course on effective communication that I was running, even though there was ample evidence throughout the day from his interactions with other participants that he was far from a good listener. So, the first point to emphasize is that we should not take listening for granted – many people are not as good at listening as they think they are – especially, as with I-it interactions above, they are tired, distracted, in a hurry or otherwise not at their best.

One very important approach to listening is *dadirri* listening. This concept derives from Australian aboriginal thought and is best characterized by the idea of 'listening with your heart'. It is about not just hearing what the other person says, but fully engaging with that person and fully appreciating what they are trying to convey (which, of course, fits nicely with the idea of I-Thou interactions).

This is an important extension of the well-established idea of *active* listening. At root, what this is about is not only listening, but actually showing you are listening – for example, through appropriate eye contact, nodding in the right places and so on. Feeding back what has been said can also be very useful – for example: 'Let me check I have got this straight: what you are saying is that ...', followed by a concise summary of what you have understood them to have said.

As we have noted, a central component of good practice in social work is trust, respect and credibility. Active listening will help to establish these important elements, whereas not being seen to listen can seriously undermine them. Effective listening is therefore doubly important: do it well and reap the benefits or fail to do it and pay the hefty price.

It can be useful to do some 'people watching' and note who listens and who doesn't, who shows they are listening and who doesn't. You may be surprised to note how often people are just not listening to each other, or, if they are, they are not showing it. How do you know someone is listening? How can you tell? How can you tell when someone is not listening? If you bear all this in mind, you will be much better equipped to get the benefits of being a good listener.

Getting the tone right

In my *Effective Communication* book (Thompson, 2018b), I make the point that, as well as verbal and nonverbal communication, we have what is known as 'paralanguage' – that is, the things that go alongside the language we use. This would include:

- *Tone of voice* How harsh or soft a tone is can make a big difference, as can how authoritative or wavering our voice may be.

- *Pace* Nervousness can make people speak quickly, while feeling down or depressed can lead to people speaking slowly. Tuning in to pace can give us a lot of useful information, but we also have to make sure that the pace we speak at is appropriate in the circumstances.

- *Loudness* Getting our volume level is important too, not so quiet that people struggle to hear us, but not so loud that they may feel intimidated.

- *Pitch* High-pitched speech can come across as nervous and lacking in authority, so not good for our credibility.

- *Register* This is the technical term for particular 'codes' we may use – for example, professional jargon, slang or child-centred language. Making sure that we are using the right 'code' is important (for example, formal language for formal circumstances and informal language for informal ones).

It is therefore important that we have sufficient self-awareness to be able to tune in to the paralanguage that we are using. The idea that 'it's not what you say, it's the way that you say it' may be a well-worn cliché, but it still has more than a grain of truth to it. Paralanguage can make a highly significant difference to how people perceive us, how they relate to us and to what extent they take note of what we are saying.

Nonverbal communication

We have already noted the importance of nonverbal communication. It is particularly important when it comes to human connection. This is because it is so powerful in its impact – we pay so much attention to the signals that are given off. For example, if someone comes across as nervous, we are likely to have little faith in them.

Consider the following two scenarios:

- You meet someone for the first time and, within just a few minutes, you feel very comfortable with them, you seem to have connected very effectively already.

- You meet someone for the first time and, within just a few minutes, you feel quite uncomfortable; there is just something about them that doesn't seem right.

The chances are that, in both cases, it is nonverbal communication that is making all the difference. In the first scenario it is likely to be a high level of nonverbal skill on that person's part that is putting you at your ease. This may not be the only factor, but it is highly likely to be a significant one. Likewise, in the second scenario, it is likely that the person concerned is lacking in nonverbal communication skills and is doing things that rankle with you: avoiding eye contact (or making too much eye contact and coming across as threatening); standing too close, and so on.

An important question to ask yourself, therefore, is: where between these two extremes would locate yourself? In other words, how would you rate your level of skill in using body language effectively to make that all-important human connection?

An important element of effectiveness in this regard is 'self-monitoring'. This is an aspect of self-awareness. It refers to checking from time to time how you are coming across. The key to this is getting the balance right. If you check too often you will come across as self-conscious and nervous, thereby creating obstacles to making that connection. If you do not check often enough, you may not realize that you are not coming across as positively as you could. For example, you will no doubt have come across people who talk very loudly in public settings and do not realize they are annoying people around them – no self-monitoring has been happening. Similarly, someone who talks at great length about him- or herself may not realize that the other people involved lost interest some time ago – the clues are not being picked up.

 Don't underestimate the importance of nonverbal communication. It is doubly important, because getting it right can make such a positive difference, but getting it wrong can have such a negative impact.

Empathy

Empathy is the balance between sympathy and apathy. Sympathy involves sharing someone's feelings. If they are sad, you are sad; if they are disappointed, you are disappointed, and so on. This is not something we can realistically sustain over time in social work. We would wear ourselves out (and wear ourselves down too) if we were to be experiencing the range of feelings we encounter in our work.

Apathy is at the other end of the spectrum – it involves having no feelings, lacking compassion, and therefore being a potential liability when working with people who are distressed, suffering, anxious, confused, grieving and so on. Indeed, apathy is generally a sign of a dangerous level of burnout.

Between these two problematic extremes is empathy. This is where we recognize people's feelings (that is, we exercise a suitable level of sensitivity), and we respond appropriately to them by trying to be as supportive and constructive as we reasonably can.

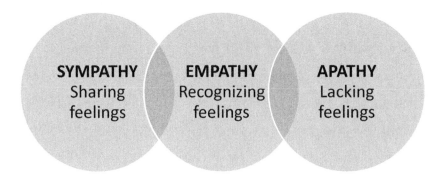

As the diagram above shows, though, these areas overlap. There is a degree of shared territory between sympathy and empathy. What this means is that some degree of sympathy is inevitable at times – we are human, after all. However, it is important that we do not move altogether from the empathy sphere to the sympathy one and leave ourselves open to emotional overload. Similarly, there is a degree of overlap between empathy and apathy, which means that at times, we may be too tired or too overloaded (perhaps with our own emotional life challenges) and thereby let a little bit of apathy creep in (although it is to be hoped that we will be professional enough not to let this cause any problems for others, whether clients, carers or colleagues).

Clearly, then, empathy is what we need to aim for, as that forms an important foundation for the human connection is at the heart of our work.

Social factors

Sociology has long since taught us that we will get a distorted picture if we focus on individuals in isolation without taking into consideration the wider social context. This applies just as much to human connection as it does to any other aspect of our work.

In view of this we will need to consider whether any of the following factors (alone or in combination) are likely to be of significance:

- *Gender* There are differences in how men and women use language (Mooney and Evans, 2015) and there are also different cultural norms around behaviour and social interactions. Breaking these 'rules' can create a great deal of tension.

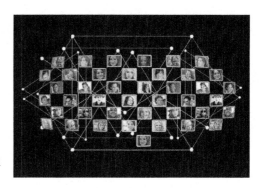

- *Race/ethnicity* Cultural differences will also apply in terms of ethnicity, of course, and we should not forget that racism, or fear and suspicion about it, can also play a major part.

- *Class* Sometimes the differences between one person's class background and another's can be immense, potentially creating obstacles to positive interactions. Anyone paying no attention to such matters is ignoring something that can be quite significant.

- *Age* Generational differences plus the prevalence of ageist assumptions can create barriers if we are not careful, as can internalized oppression whereby some older people see themselves as less worthy.

- *Language* Over half of the world's population is bilingual and not everyone speaks the mainstream language of the society they live in. Sensitivity to language differences is therefore essential.

- *Religion* Unwittingly failing to respect someone's religion will stand in the way of human connection, as will sectarianism and Islamophobia in many circumstances.

This is not a comprehensive list, of course, but it should be enough to make the point that we need to avoid too narrow a focus and make sure that we are taking account of wider social factors.

Authentic Connection Exercise

Watch people interacting, whether in real life, on television or in the cinema. See if you can spot which interactions are of an I-Thou kind and which are more like I-it. What makes the difference between the two? See if you can pin it down to specific concrete differences in how people relate to one another. Once you have done that, think about how this can help you when it comes to establishing authentic connections.

14. Working with families

For the most part, even people living on their own are part of a family, if only in the sense that the vast majority will have been brought up in a family and the 'imprint' of that family will still be with them (in terms of their identity and their outlook on the world, for example). So, the family, as a social institution, can be relevant whether we are working with individuals on their own, individuals as part of families and even groups. How a family operates will be highly influential for its members – often in very positive ways, but at times in very detrimental ways.

In this section, therefore, we consider some of the practice implications of working in a society that places so much emphasis on family life.

Family ideology

The term 'family' is a highly ambiguous term. It can refer to our parents and siblings (family of origin), our current family household, our 'extended' family and even just to children (as in, 'Do you have family?'). It can be helpful, then, when using the term in different contexts, to be clear about who or what we are actually referring to.

It is commonly assumed that to live in families is a 'natural' thing to do, with its roots in biology. However, this assumption runs the risk of oversimplifying a complex picture. While, as human beings, we are indeed biological creatures, we are not purely biological beings – we are also strongly influenced by psychological, social (cultural and structural) and spiritual factors. Conventional perceptions of the family are, of course, an ideology and, as such represent power relations.

We need to be aware of this wider picture because:

- How families relate to one another, what is expected of families, and even what counts as being 'a family member' vary from culture to culture. Such variations will include class, regional and religious differences. If we assume that 'family life' is a standardized, one-size-fits-all phenomenon, we will not be doing justice to the complexities involved and will be failing in our duty of ethnically sensitive or culturally competent practice.

- How one person experiences family life can be very different from how another experiences it, even within the same family. We therefore need to make sure that we are not making misleading assumptions about what it means to be a member of a family.

- Family ideology, in the sense of the conventional rosy view of the family, will tend to highlight the positives of family life and downplay the negatives and problems associated with many people's experiences of family life, such as physical, sexual and emotional abuse, neglect, bullying, financial exploitation, and so on. The family can also be seen as playing a major part in the maintenance of inequality and discrimination – for example, by reinforcing unequal gender roles and possibly inculcating racist attitudes towards minority groups. Indeed, family experiences play a major part in shaping our worldview.

In considering the family aspect of our practice in social work we therefore need to be aware of the dangers of uncritically adopting the dominant family ideology. Once again, critically reflective practice is what we need to be aiming for.

Our own family experiences (family of origin plus current family household) are likely to have been a profound influence on us and will have shaped our sense of normality. We must not allow this to lead us to assume that everyone's family experiences were like ours.

Family problems and solutions

Families can be a wonderful source of warmth, security, fun, encouragement, support and, of course, love. However, it would be naïve not to recognize that families can also, at times, be a source of great pain, suffering, distress, trauma, violence and abuse. Families will also be places of conflict from time to time (or much of the time in some cases) and, while such conflicts will often be managed perfectly well and can even be positive on occasion, there will also be circumstances where the conflict is doing major harm – for example, by destroying self-esteem and self-respect, instilling fear and defensiveness and potentially generating considerable anxiety and depression.

Family members can become very adept at keeping such problems hidden. In order to avoid stigma and shame, both perpetrators of problems and the people on the receiving end of such difficulties can work hard to 'keep the lid on things', with the result that such problems can remain hidden from view –  thereby reinforcing the rosy view of the family, the distorted perspective that sees the positives of family life, but fails to notice the negatives, even though those negatives will be devastating for many people.

In social work, though, we are likely to have a much more balanced view, as it is likely that family-based problems will feature a great deal in our work. However, what we need to bear in mind is that other people who have not witnessed the negatives of family life may have a very different perspective. For example, it will generally be the case than the general public will greatly underestimate the prevalence of both child abuse and the abuse of vulnerable adults. I remember once being a speaker at a women's community group and quoting official figures about the number of children deemed to be at risk of abuse. Several members of the group felt that the figures were somehow wrong or overestimated, while those who were more prepared to trust the figures were visibly shocked. And, of course, those were just the figures relating to child abuse, and therefore they did not take account of the other myriad problems that so many families face.

While there is clearly a need to counterbalance what is often called the 'sunshine breakfast' model of the family presented in the media and 'wholesome' family dramas, with the more realistic picture that includes so many negatives, we should not lose sight of the positives that are also involved. Indeed, our work will often involve seeking to capitalize on those positives – for example, in terms of organizing kinship care when it becomes impossible or too risky for a child to remain in the care of their natural parent(s).

So, what we need, then, is a balanced approach to the family, one that recognizes both its strengths and its weaknesses, its pluses and its minuses. We need to avoid the unhelpful extremes of having a naïve, rosy view of the family, while also not going to the opposite extreme of being cynically negative about what family life can offer. Families can be problems, but they can also be solutions.

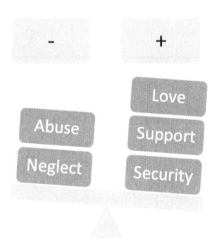

Family scripts

I have already made the point that families tend to be huge influences on us (even if we reject the 'messages' from our family, we are still being influenced by them in the very process of rejecting them). This influence pervades family life in a number of ways, but one of the strongest and most effective ways this happens is through what are known as 'family scripts'.

These are not word-for-word scripts in the theatre or cinema sense, but it does owe much to the drama analogy. A script in this sense refers to fairly standardized interactions within families. For example, consider the scenario where a teenager has yet again stayed out later than instructed. It is not too difficult to imagine a 'prosecution and defence' script in which the parent(s) adopt the role of prosecution and the teenager pleads a defence.

Different families will have different scripts, but the process of developing such institutionalized ways of interacting will apply to most if not all families. It is important to be aware of this because:

- These patterns can be causing problems – for example, where there is a process of scapegoating going on (that is, one member –usually the weakest – being blamed for what is going wrong in the family).

- Introducing new, more constructive patterns, can be part of the way in which we can help a family (as is often the case in family therapy).

- In many situations, being able to make sense of these script patterns can be a very important part of our assessment.

- Conflicts in families will often revolve around such scripts.

To identify family scripts we can rely on our observation skills – that is, we can watch carefully the interactions within the family when we get chance. This is another reason what we need analytical skills, in the sense that we need to be able to identify patterns, to pick out what is happening while it is happening. However, it is important to acknowledge that it can take time to develop the observational and analytical skills to spot such patterns and scripts, so do not be too harsh on yourself if you find this quite difficult at first.

But, it isn't just about direct observation. We can also learn a lot by asking the right questions, by teasing out from the family how they handle certain situations, how they deal with certain issues. There is an extensive family therapy literature base that can be helpful in working out what those questions might be, but working with experienced colleagues can also be of great value.

Power dynamics

Each of the two words in this subtitle is important, but especially when put together. 'Dynamics' is a significant term when it comes to families. This is because families are not static entities – they are constantly changing and developing, due to perpetual interactions within the family and between the family and the outside world, the wider context. Power will also be important as it is ever-present in human interactions, and families are no exception. Power is, amongst other things, a matter of relations of dominance and subordination.

 There will, of course, be power differences between adults and children in families, as well as issues of patriarchy (literally, 'the law of the father') to consider.

We need to combine the two words, power and dynamics, to recognize that families are a site of constant interactions and negotiations, and these will be characterized by power. For example, some family problems can arise from children having claimed power that they are not mature enough to handle yet. Similarly, the adults involved may struggle to use the power they have effectively (to exercise authority in a parenting role, for example), while the abuse of power will be an issue in relation to domestic violence, child abuse and the abuse of vulnerable adults.

In addition, there can be problems because of confusion over power, with certain individuals being reluctant to take on particular roles or activities because a degree of power is involved and they feel uncomfortable with that (family financial management, for example). What is needed, then, on our part, is a sensitivity to these power dynamics – in a sense, the ability to 'read' those dynamics, which takes us back again to observation skills, analytical skills and, of course, critically reflective practice.

We should also not forget that, once we enter the family scenario, we become part of those power dynamics – especially if one or more family members try to draw us into whatever power play(s) they are engaging in.

Conclusion

So, what we have seen in this section is that:

- Families can influence people even when they are not living in a family ('my family lives on in my head and my heart', as one elderly woman living on her own once told me);

- Families can be sources of problems as well as solutions, so we need to be wary of buying in to the dominant ideology of the family that presents a solely positive picture of family life;

- Families develop largely set patterns of interaction (often referred to as 'scripts') and an awareness of these can be useful in trying to help and support families and/or individual members; and

- Families involve power dynamics, and there is much to be gained by being able to 'tune in' to what these are.

Working with Families Exercise

What can you learn from your own family experiences that could be helpful in your work? In particular, what 'family scripts' are you aware of? You might find it helpful to discuss these issues with family members and/or colleagues.

15. Working with groups

Groupwork is not as popular an option in social work as it once was, but this is a great pity, as working in groups can be highly effective, producing some very positive results. So, if you have never undertaken groupwork, are not aware of its value and are therefore considering skipping this section, I would urge you not to. Even if you are not in a position to use groupwork now in your current role, being aware of at least the basics of what groupwork is all about will put you in a stronger position for recognizing suitable opportunities in the future.

Why use groupwork?

Much of our lives is spent in a group context, whether in teams and professional associations at work; in families outside of work; at college, university or other learning group; or in clubs, associations or friendship groups in our leisure time. Such groups can be very influential, and, like families, they can be sources of problems or solutions and involve power dynamics.

The value of groupwork is that you can bring people together who have similar problems and/or similar circumstances and work towards: (i) helping them collectively, rather than individually (which can mean a very effective use of time and scarce resources); and (ii) helping them to help one another (a benefit that can go on long after any groupwork sessions have finished.

Group work can be used in a variety of settings and contexts:

- With young people who are having difficulties – in relation to problematic drug use, for example;

- With people experiencing mental health problems – around anxiety and depression, for example.

- With parents who are struggling with the demands of bringing up their children in difficult circumstances; and

- With people with learning disabilities to help them develop their social and life skills.

This is far from an exhaustive list, but it paints a picture of the wide variety of possibilities for the use of groupwork.

Perhaps the most compelling reason for doing groupwork is that it can be so empowering. For example, if group members realize that other group members are struggling with what they have been struggling with, they can feel reassured and thereby feel more confident and in control. The bonds between members that can be formed are also likely to be empowering. In fact, the more you learn about groupwork, the more you are likely to wonder why it is not used much more than it actually is.

Planning and purpose

Groups will often operate on an informal unplanned basis, but if you are intending to use groupwork as a social work method, then it is important to have a clear plan and a clear purpose. Let's begin with purpose: What are you hoping to achieve by using groupwork? It is essential to have a clear focus, otherwise a great deal of time, effort and energy can be wasted, with little to show for it. People can also easily become disengaged if they do not see any purpose to their involvement. We shall return to the question of clarity about what we are trying to achieve in Section 23.

So, clarifying the purpose in precise terms is a key part of the planning. Other important factors to consider will be:

- *Who is to be involved?* Who should the participants be? Why? How many in the group? Why? Sole facilitator or small team? Why?

- *Open or closed?* Can new members join further down the line or is membership restricted to the initial group? This will depend on the nature and the focus of the group.

- *Short term or long term?* Will it be a fixed-term group to cover a specific set of issues (for example, a parenting education group) or will it be ongoing for as long as there is a need (a grief support group, for example)?

- *Discussion or more?* Some groups will be entirely discussion based, while others will involve exercises, games or other activities geared towards increasing awareness and encouraging involvement.

This is not an exhaustive list either, but it does present a good foundation to build on.

Groups in general can do a great deal of good or a great deal of harm, depending on various sets of circumstances, but especially as a result of the actions (or inactions) of any leaders that there may be. The same applies to especially constituted groups for social work practice purposes – we can do harm through groups, especially if we are poorly prepared and have not thought the issues through. However, it is important to emphasize that groupwork can be of immense value and make a hugely positive difference, provided that we approach the work professionally.

Much can be gained from seeking out people who have experience of groupwork and especially of planning groups to see what insights can be gained from what they have done, looking at both things that have worked well and things that could have gone better.

Imagine being part of a specially established group and having high hopes that it can help you solve a problem or meet a need that you are currently wrestling with. Imagine too that the leader(s) of this group appear to have done little preparation and have no clear idea of what they are trying to achieve by holding the group sessions. How much faith would you have in the leaders and thus in the group?

Managing the dynamics

Groups are, in a sense, sets of dynamics – that is, they consist of interactions between and across members (no interactions = no group). The way groupwork operates as a social work method is through influencing those interactions in a positive direction. Being able to influence or manage the group dynamics is therefore at the heart of effective groupwork. It should be helpful, then, to explore what is involved in managing group dynamics.

The first point to emphasize is that we once again need analytical skills; we need to be able to 'read' the dynamics, to spot what is going on as people interact. This can involve various elements, including the following:

- Who is participating? Why? Who is not? Why not?
- Who supports whom? Why?
- Who attacks or undermines whom? Why?
- Are any alliances forming? What? Why?
- What topics or issues generate most discussion? Why?
- When do 'flat spots' occur? Why?

We could continue this list for quite some time, as groups are rich in complex dynamics. The more groupwork we do, the more we should be able to spot. But, to begin with, we should be able to tune in to some of the basic interactive processes that are going on.

When it comes to reading the dynamics, this is where having a co-facilitator can be really useful, partly because he or she can see what is happening when you are engaged with one or more members (and vice versa), and partly because there can be some very useful post-session debriefings in which you can help each other.

This is also, of course, an opportunity to use your social work knowledge and skills (underpinned by social work values, of course) – for example, in terms of:

- *Communication and interpersonal skills* Being able to put people at their ease; helping them to feel comfortable and welcome.

- *Negotiation and conflict management skills* Being able to challenge without threatening, to address tensions constructively.

- *Emotional intelligence* Having sufficient, knowledge, understanding and sensitivity to be able to handle the emotional issues involved.

There is much to be learned by watching groups in action, whether in real life, on television or in cinema. Every group interaction will be unique, but there will also be discernible sets of patterns that can help to give us a foundation of learning that we can build on over time. The key is to look for patterns, things that keep recurring, then you can start to ask why that is happening. That will then enable you to think about what are the underlying processes that are going on here, so that you are better equipped to strengthen the positive processes and address the negative ones.

Rising to the challenges

Running a group can be a very positive and rewarding experience. However, it would be naïve to imagine that there will be no problems or challenges involved. It's therefore important to give some thought to how things can go wrong and how we might be able to address any such problems. Of course, in the space available we can't expect to cover them all, but what we can cover should none the less be helpful:

➢ *Non-engagement* It may be a lack of confidence, a lack of clarity about what is expected of them or various other reasons, but it is not uncommon to find that some people are very reluctant to contribute – they just don't seem to be engaging at all. This can especially be the case when individuals are attending because they have to (a group of young offenders, for example) and are not really committed and are thus quite cynical about the whole thing. They may also be anxious about the possibility of conflict arising, especially if they are aware that they disagree with one or more group members on certain issues or approaches. There are, as is so often the case in social work, no simple or formula solutions to this, but there are none the less various things we can do:

   o Make sure everyone feels welcome and valued.
   o Make sure what is expected of people is crystal clear.
   o Give everyone ample encouragement to join in.

➢ *Hijacking* Some participants may try to take over and use the group for their own ends at the expense of the other participants (and at your expense too, of course, in terms of what you are trying to do). For example, one person may try to use the group to bolster their own ego or find other ways of serving their own interests. In such circumstances the problem needs to be tackled sooner, rather than later, as the longer the hijacking goes on, the worse the damage will be. The situation will have to be handled carefully and sensitively by finding ways of challenging what is happening without becoming confrontational. As a last resort, it may be necessary to ask the person concerned to leave the group, but this should indeed be a last resort, as it is a big – and potentially risky – step to take. But, it is essential that something is done to address the problem, as failure to do so is highly likely to undermine – if not destroy – your credibility.

➤ *Sabotage* This is similar to hijacking, but also subtly different. Hijacking is where one or more members are spoiling things for others by serving their own interests, whereas sabotage is geared towards spoiling things for its own sake – for example, because the saboteur is not committed to the process, is mistrustful of it or cynical about the whole endeavour. The object of the exercise is not to benefit from it except by getting the perverse satisfaction of ruining things for others. At times, such sabotage attempts can be a way of challenging the group leader's authority (much as a child would do in testing out an adult's authority). The challenges of handling this sort of problem will be the same as dealing with hijacking – the same issues apply.

➤ *Conflict* As we shall see in Section 20, conflict can be a good thing at times, but it can also do a great deal of harm. Some degree of conflict is inevitable, but the key issue will be how (effectively or otherwise) it is dealt with. Groupwork can help to identify conflict issues and help resolve them, enabling people to move forward positively. However, it is also possible that conflict that is not well managed can spoil a group by creating tensions that prevent participants from joining in and encourages them to be defensive – a clear barrier to empowerment. It is therefore important to ensure that: (i)  conflicts are recognized (the earlier, the better); and (ii) addressed constructively, rather than be allowed to smoulder or fester.

What is really important in rising to these challenges is the confidence and credibility we discussed in Section 3. Without these we will really struggle to win the trust of group participants and be well placed to influence group dynamics in a positive direction.

Groupwork can indeed be challenging and should not be undertaken lightly. However, with proper preparation and, ideally, the support of an experienced colleague, it can also be highly effective and enriching for all involved.

*** KEY POINT ***

Much of human experience occurs in a group context. Whether or not we intend to engage in groupwork as a social work method, it is important that we have a good awareness of how groups operate (including teams and and multidisciplinary partnerships) and are prepared to carry on learning to develop that understanding further.

Working with Groups Exercise

Think about the groups, formal or informal, that you have been involved in at various times during your life. Make a list of the positive things that you have seen emerge form groups, then compare that with a list of the negatives associated with groups. You should then be able to think about how you can strengthen the positives and guard against the negatives.

16. Working with communities

For the most part, social work involves working *in* communities, but in this section we are going to look at some of the practice issues that arise when we are working *with* communities. In the early days of my career, it was common to describe social work in terms of three main 'branches': casework, groupwork and community work. However, over the years,  the focus of social work has narrowed considerably, with the major focus now being on casework, with only occasional use of groupwork and little or no community work. This is a great pity, as there is much that can be done in working with communities that can make such a positive difference to the community itself and its members. This narrowing is largely due to the 'consumerist' focus that has arisen as part of neoliberalism (see Section 23). However, as we shall see, the new emphasis on co-production is reaffirming the value of having a greater community focus.

Why work with communities?

Like families and groups, communities can be sources of both problems and solutions. Community-based social work can therefore play an important role in addressing problems and capitalizing on the potential solutions.

Like the family ideology with its rosy view of family life, a romantic view of communities is also quite commonplace. The reality once again is a mixture of positives and negatives. We therefore need to avoid the unhelpful extremes of: (i) seeing the community as a panacea that can cure everyone's ills; and (ii) seeing the community as nothing but a source of discrimination, stigma, exclusion and distress (all of which it can be at times, of course). The idea of working with communities is based on having a good understanding of how community issues can both help and hinder, depending on the circumstances – this is again part of holistic thinking, being able to look beyond just the individual circumstances.

 Beware of the common mistake of getting drawn into the specific circumstances of the individual and/or family and losing sight of the community as a potential source of: (i) problems; and (ii) solutions.

Important reasons for working with communities include (but are not limited to):

- A lot of useful preventative work can be done, nipping problems in the bud.

- Getting community members involved in helping others can help not only the recipients of that support, but also the providers (boosting self-esteem by helping people to feel useful, for example).

- Using informal support networks can be less stigmatizing than support from statutory authorities (and is likely to generate less resistance in most cases).

- There is a lower level of risk of dependency creation.

The importance of working in partnership is a long-standing idea in social work. However, it is now increasingly being extended into what has come to be known as 'co-production'. This refers to the bringing together of expertise, skills, resources, energy and commitment with a view to achieving agreed positive outcomes. What these outcomes are will vary from situation to situation, but the principle remains the same: it is better and more effective for people paid to address social issues and problems to work jointly with people affected by those problems in order to develop solutions.

Examples of co-production could include:

- Parents of young people affected by illicit drug use pooling resources to support one another and their respective families, with guidance and further support from the statutory authorities.

- Community members and statutory authorities working together to identify support needs for older people, match these against existing resources, identify shortfall and explore funding options for addressing that shortfall.

- Developing a scheme whereby older, more experienced parents support teenage parents with a view to preventing the need for statutory intervention and for reducing concerns about child welfare and child protection.

 The list could go on, and that is partly the appeal of co-production, it has great potential to be creative and innovative, rather than getting stuck in tramlines. What should be clear, then, is that a community focus has the potential to be very empowering for all concerned.

I have spoken to a number of social workers (on training courses, for example) who have expressed considerable anxiety about working with communities, and I can understand that it could be daunting for people who are not used to it. However, once you do get used to it, it is much easier to keep any such anxieties in proportion and not let them get in the way of the opportunities communities offer.

Capacity building

The notion of 'capacity building' is doubly significant. It can refer to what is done to strengthen communities in various ways, but it can also apply to how communities, in the right circumstances, can build the capacity of their members.

This will normally involve various schemes and projects targeted to what have been identified as the most important needs and the most significant problems. For example, if a particular community has a problem with high levels of anti-social behaviour on the part of teenagers, resources may be invested in providing more socially positive activities with a view to reducing the destructive behaviours. This is not simply a matter of pouring money into an area with high levels of social problems. Much can be done by working with local community members to capitalize on the (human) resources already available. This is often referred to as community organizing, community facilitation or even community empowerment.

Social workers can play a part in such work when the circumstances allow. But, even where there is no opportunity to participate in such work, we may still be able to make use of any such projects or activities in working with a particular individual or family or for a groupwork project.

The current emphasis on co-production fits well with this picture. It involves looking more holistically at the situations we encounter to see whether there are opportunities for interested parties ('stakeholders', to use the technical term) to work together to achieve common goals.

To a large extent, co-production is a reaction against the 'consumerism' that has developed as a result of the dominance of neoliberal policies that emphasize the role of the 'free' market and the limiting of the role of the state in public services (to be discussed further in Section 24). One of the consequences of neoliberalism has been a major focus on providing (or commissioning) services, hence the term 'consumerism'. This runs counter to the traditional idea of social work as largely a problem-solving activity geared towards empowerment. Co-production therefore reflects social work's role of problem solving and empowerment – specifically by finding ways of developing empowering partnerships around particular issues or sets of problems. This is very much at the heart of community social work.

 Beware of getting stuck in a narrow perspective where you just see individuals and families. Sociology teaches us that individuals and families are part of wider communities and we will miss out on potential sources of help and support if we lose sight of this.

Effective networking

An important concept in terms of community social work is that of social capital. The French sociologist, Pierre Bourdieu, wrote about the importance of having what we could call 'social resources'. This refers to the people we know (especially people who would be in a position to help and support us if need be); organizations we may be members of or whose resources we have access to; and so on. The extent of social capital a person has can make a huge difference to their well-being or quality of life. It is no coincidence that the older people who come to the attention of social services are so often the older people who have little by way of social capital – for example, no supportive relatives in the area.

Jordan (2007) writes about the 'interpersonal economy' by which he means that human interactions create 'social goods' (parallel with how the money economy creates 'economic goods' or wealth). Such interactions help to create meaning and to give people a sense of social worth. As such, they can make a major contribution to well-being.

It is also important to note that social interactions can either enhance or diminish well-being, be empowering or disempowering. Indeed, social work can be understood as, in large part, an activity that involves seeking to minimize destructive interactions and maximize positive ones.

Networking is a helpful way of supporting people in developing greater levels of social capital. Rather than focusing narrowly and exclusively on individual cases, community social work can make a positive difference by: (i) identifying local networks of people (formal or informal) that could be useful sources of support;

(ii) connecting individuals, families and groups to those networks as appropriate and where possible; and (iii) playing a part, alongside other community professionals in developing networks where gaps have been identified.

Over the years many people have said to me that they like the idea of community social work, but they simply do not have time to get involved in community issues. I have always responded to those comments in the same way, by saying that perhaps we would have fewer individual cases to take up our time if we devoted more time to enhancing community resources and drawing more effectively on what is already out there. What has emerged from many training courses I have run and consultancy projects I have been involved in is a realization that so often people just assume that there is little or nothing available without actually checking – it is as if they are relying on a stereotype, and a dangerous one at that, as it creates and reinforces a gap between formal statutory provision and informal community or voluntary sector provision.

Given the difficulties of switching from a consumerist casework model to a community social work one, clearly it is going to work much better if done collectively, with team and organizational backing. However, even where this is lacking, there is still much that individual practitioners can do by thinking in broader community terms.

Conclusion

Community social work is certainly not a panacea. However, in earlier times when there was a much stronger emphasis on the community context of people's lives, there was much to be gained from being able to draw on community resources and seeking to enhance those resources where necessary. We are now starting to see a resurgence of interest in communities in general (the increasing prevalence of social enterprises, for example) and community social work in particular, and that is very much to be welcomed.

It is important to emphasize, though, that we should not see it cynically as simply a process of trying to shift responsibilities for helping and supporting from social workers to communities (especially as there would be gender equality issues involved here, given that an uncritical approach to community capacity building can easily become a process of exploiting women).

It is about social workers working *with* communities to help develop optimal levels of support and assistance, particularly for the most vulnerable groups in those communities. This type of partnership can be invaluable when handled well.

Working with Communities Exercise

What steps can you take to gain a better awareness of what is available in your local community? Where can you find relevant information? Who might the key people be to make contact with? What could possibly be done to develop new community resources where there are gaps?

17. Residential work

A major feature of social work over the decades has been a commitment to keeping people within the community as far as possible and thereby keeping people out of institutional care for as long as possible. This is largely out of recognition that people are generally likely to fare better within their own homes and their own communities.

However, there will often be times where this is either not possible or not desirable. It can be not possible where someone's needs for care cannot be met within their own home, family or community setting – for example, where someone has reached a point whereby the severity of dementia means that they can no longer be left safely to their own devices, even with an extensive package of community care support measure being in place. It can be undesirable when someone – a child, for example – is being abused within their own home, and so it becomes necessary to remove them from that home for their own safety.

Normally, foster care would be the first choice in such circumstances, but there will be times when either foster care is not available or there are reasons why

residential care might be more appropriate (some children fare better outside of a family context, particularly if their experiences of family life have been very negative, and so they have a negative approach to family-based care – in such cases, residential care can be a much better alternative).

So, whether you work in residential care or your role involves referring people (adults or children) to a residential setting, it is important that you have a good understanding of some of the key issues relating to residential care – and that is precisely what this section is all about.

Home or institution?

Family life is highly valued in our society, as we noted earlier. But, what we also noted is that families can be highly problematic at times, and so alternatives can be very helpful in the right circumstances. By the same token, residential care is generally seen negatively as 'institutional' care and therefore to be avoided wherever possible. However, just as family life has its less well-publicized facets, residential care has many positives that are often disregarded. It is therefore important that we do not operate on the basis of a rigid, oversimplified stereotype along the lines of 'family good, residential care bad'. The reality is much more complex than that.

The notion of 'institution' implies a number of unfavourable features:

- Run for the convenience of the staff, not the health and well-being of the residents.
- Heavily routinized and standardized, with little or no variety or spontaneity.
- Minimalist – relying on the cheapest food and 'skimping' on other expenditure.
- Potentially or actually abusive, with little or no respect or dignity being shown.

However, it is essential that we realize that none of these is intrinsic to residential care – that is, none of them is a necessary feature of such care. Each one reflects bad practice in social care provision.

So, whether we are providing residential care, commissioning it or referring people to it, we need to bear in mind that none of these concerns is to be expected, none should be seen as 'par for the course'.

Residential care, whether for children or adults should not be 'institutional' in this negative sense, and there is no reason why it has to be that. In my career I have come across examples of very well-run, 'homely' establishments that prove that the negatives associated with residential care are not inevitable. Sadly, I have also come across examples of where such problems are alive and well.

What makes the difference in practical terms between those two extremes is how time and space are managed, and that is what we are going to focus on in a moment. However, first there are some values issues that need to be clarified. The first of these relates to ageism. Ageism involves discrimination on the grounds of age. While it tends to be used mainly to refer to discrimination against older people, we should not forget that age-related discrimination towards children and older people is also quite common (especially relating to children and young people who are 'in care'). When we consider residential care, we need to be sure that we are operating in anti-ageist ways – that is, that we are not allowing discriminatory actions, attitudes, assumptions or language to stand in the way of good practice. Ageism, if we allow it to, will strip people of their dignity and autonomy.

 The second values issue relates to how staff are treated. Where there is authentic leadership, effective management and a commitment to workplace well-being, there are likely to be few staffing problems to address. However, where there is poor or non-existent leadership, ineffectual management and no genuine commitment to ensuring staff are well treated, a whole array of problems can arise: low morale, high levels of sickness absence, high staff turnover, staff recruitment problems, sabotage and even abusive behaviours, whether towards residents or towards other employees (bullying and harassment).

Clearly, if either or both of these values issues is not being managed effectively, it is highly unlikely that positive, high-quality care will be the result, and indeed much more likely that the institutional negatives we mentioned will be to the fore.

Consequently, any consideration of residential care must take account of the central role of values.

Time and space

When I have run training courses in the past on residential care I (and the participants) have found it helpful to think in terms of time and space, as these two ideas capture much of what is important in residential care, so these are what we are going to look at now.

Time

It can be useful to think of this in two ways:

(i)   The time process in terms of beginning, middle and end – that is, how people are introduced to their new home, how they are looked after while they are there and how their departure is managed.

(ii)   How time is spent while they are living within the home.

Let's begin with (i) and focus on initial arrival. How will they be greeted? What will happen to make them feel welcome and at home? And these are not just the 'practical' matters: what consideration will be given to feelings of grief arising from the losses involved? Grief that is not acknowledged can be much harder to deal with. It is a cliché that initial  impressions count for so much, but – cliché or not – it holds a great deal of truth, and we would do well not to lose sight of that. It is essential that this initial introduction is handled sensitively and in a person-centred way.

The 'middle' part needs to be handled well too, of course. This may be a short time or a very long time, depending on the circumstances, but, whatever length it may turn out to be, the focus needs to be on the health and well-being of the person concerned and their specific needs. It is very easy in a setting that caters for several or more people for staff to get bogged down in routines and administrative matters and lose sight of the fact that, for the time being at least, this is someone's home that we are talking about – an important foundation of their lives, a foundation for their sense of security and so much more.

>>> Moccasins moment <<<

How would you feel if you or someone you love and care for were living in a residential setting? What would you expect as a bare minimum in terms of the setting being a proper home and not just an 'institution? What would you anticipate your feelings being if those minimum expectations were not being met?

The final stage could be a positive return home in some circumstances or, at the other extreme, it could be through death. Whatever the cause of the stay in residential care coming to an end, care needs to be taken to ensure that it is handled well. If someone is returning home, moving on to another residential setting or perhaps to foster care, there will need to be time and space for goodbyes. Seeing the process as purely an administrative one of filling in a form or two, arranging transport and so on, is highly disrespectful and a further example of very poor practice. Any work undertaken in a residential care context needs to be person centred from start to finish if we are to avoid causing unnecessary problems and ill feeling.

Where a death has occurred, careful consideration will need to be given not only to loss and grief issues, but also to such matters as preferred funeral arrangements and related matters. Such matters should have been discussed and recorded beforehand, of course. It is extremely unwise to wait until a death occurs before thinking about what is the best way to respond sensitively and professionally to the challenges involved.

In terms of (ii), the stereotype of an eldercare home with people either inactive or engaged in a limited range of simple activities should not be allowed to become the reality. A risk-averse approach to activities can be very counterproductive by limiting not only people's activities, but also their horizons.

Productive use of time, whether for children or adults is an important issue that is often given less attention than it deserves. Our day-to-day activities are part of our sense of identity and thus part of our sense of security. An unimaginative, clichéd approach to activities can do a lot of harm.

We should also remember the importance of reciprocity. People need to give as well as receive, help as well as be helped. We would therefore do well to ensure that activities include opportunities for reciprocity.

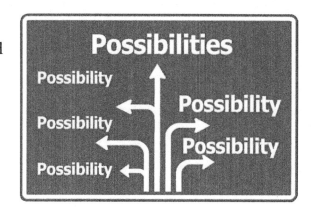

Space

It isn't just time that needs to be handled sensitively; there is also space to consider. This includes personal space in the physical sense (room décor, furnishings, availability of personal effects and so on) as well as the metaphorical sense of having one' own space and control over how it is used (access to music of their choice, for example). This would include control over how much time is spent with other people and how much is spent alone (we should not assume that constantly being with other people is what everybody wants).

Again these issues can be very significant in terms of a person's sense of self and sense of security. There is a high price to pay for neglecting them.

Conclusion

Of course, we cannot cover everything relating to residential care in such a short space, but this section should give you at least a basic understanding to build on and plenty of food for thought.

*** KEY POINT ***

Our home, whether we live alone, in a family group or in a residential setting is not only a basic part of our physical security, but also an essential pillar of our spiritual well-being.

Residential Care Exercise

If you were asked to set up a brand new residential facility for a particular client group, what would you feel were the important factors to take into account in planning it? How would you make sure it was more of a home than an institution?

18. Court work

Not all social workers will be called upon to appear in court as a mainstream part of their job. However, any social worker may be required to attend court in certain circumstances (where their employers are being sued, for example). Knowing at least the basics of court work is therefore very wise, hence this section focusing on what is involved.

We begin by looking at the main reasons social workers should be involved in court work. We then look at what is expected of us in a court setting, before focusing on the skills involved.

Why court work?

There are two sets of key issues that we need to bear in mind. First, courts revolve around the idea of justice. That is, whatever happens in a courtroom or the preparatory work geared towards a court appearance should be informed by, and committed to, achieving justice – fair outcomes for those involved. Because of this, court work has to be undertaken very carefully, with close attention to detail. Consequently, when we are involved in any form of court work, we need to focus very closely and carefully on what we are doing and the issues involved, and, in so doing, make sure that we do not lose sight of the justice concerns involved.

The second set of issues relates to *power*. Courts are very powerful places that have the potential to make a huge difference – for good or ill – to the lives of many people who are directly or indirectly involved. As social workers, of course, we are certainly not the most powerful players in that arena, but we should be very careful not to make the mistake of assuming that we have no power and only a minor role to play.

Judges, magistrates, solicitors and barristers all have powerful roles to play within the court system. However, in very many cases, their knowledge of the person, family or circumstances will depend on information provided by the social worker. We will have the opportunity to play a part in shaping their understanding and trying to make sure that they are aware of important aspects of the situation. Sound decisions cannot be made without the proper information and understanding.

Don't lose sight of the fact that social workers play an important role in court, as we have the opportunity to influence the course of the proceedings through the information and evidence we provide.

What is expected?

In dispensing justice courts go through decision-making processes, and, in the interests of fairness, those processes need to be well informed and unbiased. They therefore require evidence to be presented to them in as helpful and informative a way as reasonably possible. In this way, as social workers we are acting as a conduit between the individual or family and the decision-making apparatus of the court system. We are therefore expected to assist the court (and thereby assist the client/s in achieving justice) by providing relevant information to help establish a clear picture of the situation. This will generally be in the form of a written report, but can also involve being 'cross examined' – that is, being asked to answer questions in the actual courtroom.

In many court situations we will also have an important role in supporting the individual or family concerned. This will include giving emotional (or 'moral') support, easing tension by explaining what is going on and providing practical assistance as appropriate. This can be particularly important where children are involved in the situation.

More specific expectations will depend on the circumstances in term of what type of court situation is involved. Consider the following examples:

> *Care proceedings* Where one or more children cannot remain at home in the care of their parent(s) due to abuse, family breakdown or other valid reason, the authority of the court will normally be required in order to have the legal right to place the child with foster carers or other suitable place of residence. For the court to make the required order, it will be necessary to establish that it is in the child(ren)'s best interests to do so (in terms of their health, welfare, development, safety or a mixture of these) and that these interests cannot be secured without such an order. The court has to weigh the 'balance of probabilities' – that is, to be convinced that it is more likely than not that an order is in the child's best interests. Clearly, the court will need appropriate information and understanding of the circumstances, and that is a key part of why the social worker is there.

> *Youth justice* In recognition of the complexities and sensitivities involved in offending behaviour on the part of children and young people, there is a separate court system in which magistrates receive extra training. The aim is to find the most appropriate 'disposal' (that is, outcome or decision) with a view to balancing appropriate punishment with efforts to reduce the likelihood of further offending. Social workers and other youth justice personnel will be asked to provide reports to assist the courts. A key social work consideration is trying to keep the offender 'down tariff' – that is, to achieve the least punitive sentence. In particular, it is important to avoid custodial sentences where young people can be introduced to very negative influences and become more fully immersed in a world of crime.

> *Litigation* From time to time a client may feel so dissatisfied that they decide to sue the organization that provided social work or social care support for them – for example, where someone has been abused and they, or their carer(s), feel that not enough was done to prevent, or offer protection from, the abusive situation. In such situations the emphasis for the social worker will be on accountability. This involves being called upon to account for their

actions, provide a professional rationale for decisions made, actions taken or not taken. This can involve writing a report and/or answering questions.

These are not the only court scenarios possible, but they should give a flavour of what is expected of social workers in the court arena.

What skills are needed?

In some ways court work is a highly skilled form of practice. We do not have space to explore the full range of skills in depth, but what we can do is give an overview of some of the main ones and show why they are so important.

> *Anxiety management* A significant proportion of people find court work quite a scary undertaking. Understandably, it can generate a lot of anxiety, but it is essential that we do not allow that anxiety to get in the way of our doing our job calmly, carefully and effectively. What can make this difficult is that other people in the court arena can get anxious too – the individual or family concerned, for example. Their anxiety can be infectious if we let it, but that is the key phrase: *if we let it.* It is essential that we stay calm and help others to calm down, rather than allow their anxiety to wind us up. This is an important part of professionalism in general, but will be particularly to the fore in a court setting. When we encounter one or more people who are anxious, it is our job to make them less anxious, not to allow their anxiety to make us more anxious. Some degree of anxiety is inevitable and is in itself a good thing, but the problem comes when it is allowed to escalate, when a reasonable amount of anxiety leads to more anxiety that in turn leads to more still, and so on. Staying calm and focused is therefore essential.

> *Report-writing skills* As we shall see in the next section, report-writing skills are a fundamental part of a social worker's repertoire of skills. This is particularly the case in court work, as the information you provide in your

report will be taken on board by powerful people making one or more decisions that can have a major effect on a person's life. It is therefore essential that your report is clear and unambiguous; accurate and to the point; providing the necessary information, with no padding; unbiased; and, most of all, helpful in facilitating the decision-making process.

As I shall emphasize in Section 19, what can be helpful is to put yourself in the reader's shoes – to ask yourself: If I needed to make a decision about this situation, what information would I need? What would I need to understand? You can then use those insights to guide you in preparing your report.

➢ *Giving evidence* Your report will, in itself, constitute evidence to the court, but you may also be asked to give what is known as 'oral testimony', which simply means being asked questions in court. Any such questions are likely to involve: (i) points of clarification relating to your report; (ii) requests for further information – that is, being asked to expand on points made in your

report or to comment on matters not covered in your report; and (iii) possibly challenging your point of view – especially if there are conflicting points of view. For example, in care proceedings, a family member may adopt a different perspective from yours or may deny that certain things happened. Also, there may be conflicting views *within* a family that you may be asked to comment on.

Unfortunately, the court system is traditionally an adversarial one, which means that it is a form of theatrical battle, with one 'side' trying to do down the other 'side'. The children's legal system is intended to be less adversarial than the main court system, but my experience has been that it too can have a strong adversarial element. The main implication of this is that, in giving evidence, you may encounter some degree of resistance in the form of legal professionals trying to undermine your evidence, trying to make out that it is not reliable. It is *essential* that you do not take this personally. They have nothing against you, they are not trying to do you any harm, you are not under attack. They are just 'playing the game' of testing out how robust your evidence is. And, of course, if you have prepared your report well and kept anxiety under control, your evidence should have no problem in terms of its robustness.

Giving evidence in court has the potential to be quite a challenging and demanding experience, but it is nothing to panic about (hence the emphasis on anxiety management) and can also be a highly rewarding experience. The more you do this type of work, the less challenging it becomes and the more rewarding it can be – and the more confident you can become in tackling court work.

*** KEY POINT ***

The central role of confidence was emphasized in Section 3. If we do not have confidence in ourselves, we cannot expect others to have confidence in us.

> *Maintaining perspective* Courts are busy, pressurized places where, as we have noted, there can be a great deal of anxiety and considerable tension and uncertainty. In such circumstances it is understandable that people may lose perspective, they may lose sight of what their role is or what the object of the exercise is – that is, they may get lost in the drama and tension of the situation. In Section 23 we will see why it is important to remain clear about what our role is and what we are trying to achieve. This applies to all social work practice situations, but the court arena is one where things are more likely to go wrong than would normally be the case. In undertaking court work, we therefore need to remain clear throughout about:

- o Why is this matter going to court?
- o What decision(s) does the court need to make?
- o What is my role in this situation?

- What support do I need to give to the individual(s) or family concerned?
- What support do I need and where can I get it from?

In other words, it is essential that we do not 'lose the plot' and lose sight of what is going on or what needs to happen.

Conclusion

Understandably, courts can be anxiety-provoking places, but we should also remember that they can be extremely helpful places in terms of getting decisions made, getting access to resources and so on. The more experience we have of this type of work, the more effective and confident we can be. While we build up our experience and skills, we need to keep anxiety in check, communicate effectively (in writing and orally) and make sure we do not lose sight of what the overall process is all about and what it is intended to achieve.

Court Work Exercise

What options do you have for keeping your own anxiety under control? What can you do to help others keep their anxiety within manageable limits? Who is the person you know who best handles anxiety? How do they do it? If possible, ask them what strategies they use to stay calm.

19. Report writing and record keeping

'Too much paperwork and not enough people work' is a commonly heard refrain in social work. The burden of keeping records and writing reports is generally perceived as a negative aspect of the work. While I can fully appreciate the sentiment behind such a comment, my concern is that too often practitioners do not fully appreciate the value and significance of written work. So, in this section we are going to explore some of the key issues involved and, in doing so, clarify why effective practice in this area is central to professionalism (and why paperwork is part of people work).

Why we write

 Writing is, of course, a form of communication. What makes it particularly important is its *endurance*, in the sense that what you write today may be read by another worker (or by the client or by various others potentially) in a year's time, five years' time and even much longer from now. What is said may be forgotten just a few moments after it has been uttered, whereas what is written has the potential to be influential a very long time after it has been written – all the more reason for making sure that it is accurate, fair and helpful.

As professionals we need to keep records of our activities, partly as an aide-memoire to jog our memory as and when required, partly as a means of communicating with others (either now or in the future) to keep them in the picture, and partly for reasons of accountability (that is, of evidence of our actions and the reasons for them) so that, if called upon to do so, we can justify the steps we took (or decided not to take).

We should never lose sight of these reasons for writing, but, sadly, over the years, I have come across many examples of written work by social workers that had lost sight of one or more of these reasons for writing (for example, a record indicating what was done, but not even a hint of *why* it was done). I have seen records of decisions made, with no information about on what basis the decision was made. For someone working with the individual or family concerned at a later date it can be very unhelpful not have a grasp of why certain decisions were made.

What we should especially not lose sight of is the recognition that the paperwork is a form of professional communication and, as such, has a vitally important part to play. Consider the many widely publicized incidences where social work intervention has gone wrong – where child abuse situations have been mishandled, for example. A recurring theme across these cases is poor or non-existent communication, and, of course, in most if not all cases, much of that will have been poor or non-existent *written* communication. The tendency to see 'paperwork' as less important than the 'real' work is therefore a dangerous distortion.

What we write

Written work in social work takes many forms. There can be 'running records', day-to-day accounts of practice activities; there can be forms that need to be filled in for legal or administrative reasons – especially where financial matters are involved; and there will also be emails, letters and reports for communicating important information to others involved.

Over the years I have run very many courses on report-writing and record-keeping skills. Consistently what people have wanted to learn on those courses can be summarized in two questions. The first is: When writing, what do we include and what do we leave out? The short answer to that question is: You include what is relevant and leave out what is not. Of course, that then leads to the next question: How do you know what is relevant and what is not? And the short answer to that question is: It all depends on the purpose, on why you are writing. That should tell you, in broad outline at least, what needs to be included – what will actually serve the purpose intended by whatever it is you are writing. For example, if you are writing a report requested by a psychiatrist, you would need to ask yourself: What information do I have that will (within the bounds of confidentiality) help the psychiatrist to help the client? That will give you the basis of what you need to write.

Indeed, whatever we are called upon to write, there will be a reason for doing so, and it is very important that we bear that reason in mind, as that will be very helpful in helping us to decide what we need to write. As I mentioned in Section 18, it can be a useful exercise to put yourself in the reader's shoes and think about what, in the particular circumstances concerned, you would need to know. That should give you some ideas about what needs to be included in what you write.

How we write

There are various things we need to take into consideration when it comes to written communication. What can be helpful in this regard is to make sure that our writing is SHAPED properly, with SHAPED being an acronym for six important principles:

Succinct and accurate | Helpful and clear | Analytical | Purpose driven | Empowering | Dated

It is worth exploring each of these principles to see how they can be very useful in helping us to establish best practice in our written work. It is assumed that you already have basic writing skills that can be developed and improved over time. This framework should help you to make what you write as effective as possible in your record keeping and report writing.

➤ **S***uccinct and accurate* If we include irrelevant material, pad things out or write more fully than we need to, there is a danger that people will just skim read what we write and thereby risk missing something important, crucial even. Writing more than necessary is also a waste of time and the time of the people in future who need to wade through the irrelevant stuff to what matters. In my *People Skills* book I talk about writing 'the minimum necessary, not the maximum available'. 'The minimum necessary' means writing enough to communicate what we need to, nothing more, nothing less. In terms of the 'maximum available', just because we have information available to us does not mean we have to pass it on, as that would mean we would soon be clogged up with information that does not help. The key to being succinct, then, is being very clear about why we are writing and therefore what we need to write, rather than stuffing in as much as possible just because we can. This is, of course, an example of the need for reflective practice – we need to work out what is and what is not relevant, rather than just try to record everything in an unthinking, unfocused way.

We also need to make sure that what we write is accurate. This means that we avoid writing in vague or ambiguous ways and that we check our facts. Inaccurate or misleading information can do a lot of harm.

➤ **H***elpful and clear* For what you write to be helpful it has to be fit for purpose, so that brings us back to the need to be clear about what that purpose is: Why are you writing this? What are you trying to achieve by doing so? In effect, you need to be clear that what you are writing is doing what you need it to do.

And, of course, to be helpful, what you write has to be clear. If it is not clear to the person(s) reading it what you were trying to say, what was the point of writing it? Clarity in writing comes from:

   o *Clear thinking* If you are not clear about what you are trying to say, it isn't going to be possible to say it clearly. So, you need to get your thoughts in order before you can get your words in order.

- *Clear style* Are you writing in well-constructed sentences that are not too lengthy? (Overlong, overloaded sentences are a common problem in written work.) Are you using paragraphs effectively to break up what you are writing into manageable chunks? Are you using punctuation effectively to make it easier for the reader to digest what you are saying?

➢ **A**nalytical There is an important distinction between description and analysis. To write in a descriptive way is to provide the basic information, the 'raw data' as it were. Often, this is all that is required. However, we often need to go beyond basic description and engage in analysis. To write analytically  means not just presenting the basic information, but going beyond that to process it, to make sense of it and to comment on its significance. This is part of reflective practice, of course – not just taking situations at face value, but reflecting on them and making sense of them. Analytical writing will not just say what happened, but also offer some contribution to establishing how and why it happened. For example, in a risk assessment, there is not much point in simply listing the risk factors involved. We would need to analyse the situation much more fully, get a much better informed picture of the *significance* of those risks.

Many people struggle to write analytically at first, but it is a skill that can be developed. You might find it helpful to look at other people's writings and explore how analytical they are. If they come across as quite analytical, what is it that is giving you that impression? If they come across as not very analytical, what is missing? What could have helped make them more analytical (and therefore more useful as a written record)?

➢ **P**urpose driven I have already emphasized the importance of being clear about why you are writing something. This is because it will give you a basis for working out what you need to write (what to include and what to leave out). Knowing why you are writing something should give you a helpful understanding from which to work out precisely what you are trying to communicate.

➤ **E**mpowering Given the central role of empowerment in social work, it should not come as a surprise to learn that what we write should also be empowering. What this means is that our writing should be non-judgemental (judgemental comments in written records or a report can be highly stigmatizing, discriminatory and thus destructive). The written word can be very powerful, and so we need to make sure that the power being exercised is being used in a positive (empowering) direction, and not in a negative (oppressive) direction. This will include making sure that what we write is fair and unbiased, avoiding stereotypes or other discriminatory assumptions.

➤ **D**ated This may seem an obvious thing to say, but time and again I have come across written records that are not dated, and so working out how they fit into the overall chronology and narrative becomes very difficult if not impossible. It is therefore essential that we make sure that we attach a date to what we write.

>>> Moccasins moment <<<

If records or reports were being written about you, how important would it be to you for what is written to be fair, unbiased and non-judgemental? What would your reaction be if it were not?

This is not a comprehensive review of principles of effective written work in social work, but it is certainly a helpful foundation on which to build. If you are able to make sure that your writing is SHAPED properly, you will be well on the way to success.

 It is essential to keep on top of your writing duties. Sadly, it is not uncommon for people to get behind with their writing. This is dangerous, as the longer you leave it, the harder it is to write clearly, accurately and effectively. It also suggests you are not prioritizing effective communication.

Report Writing and Record Keeping Exercise

For this exercise what I want you to do is to review the quality of your written work. Having read Section 19, what do you see as your current strong points? How would you envisage building on them? What do you see as your areas for development? What can you do to improve on these?

20. Managing conflict

Conflict is a major part of social work, although, strangely, its significant role is rarely given the attention it deserves. Conflict can occur between ourselves and the people we serve, between ourselves and other professionals, between the people we serve and other professionals, within families, within our own organization, and in various other combinations. We can also have our own inner conflict, of course.

The better our understanding of conflict, the better equipped we will be to manage it when we encounter it (note: when, not if) and the better the results we will get for our efforts.

 Conflict is a widely misunderstood concept, and so one of the first things we will be doing in this section is exploring in more detail what conflict is all about in order to dispel some of those misunderstandings. We will then move on to look at how conflict can be understood to operate at four levels, and, finally, we shall examine a particular framework that can be useful in shaping our responses to situations that involve conflict.

Clarifying conflict

A common misunderstanding around conflict is that it involves hostility. When people say: 'I don't like conflict' what they generally mean is: 'I don't like hostility'. However, what we need to be totally clear about is that conflict normally starts long before hostility enters the picture. If we are not aware of this we will not recognize the earlier indicators of conflict and therefore not be in a position to 'nip things in the bud'. Indeed, if we wait for conflict to reach the hostility stage, we may well have missed the best opportunities to do something about that conflict.

As we shall see below (when we discuss the four levels of conflict), conflict begins with disagreement, with a difference of perspective, approach, understanding or values. These differences can be productive and helpful, or they can lead to significant problems. Being aware of such differences and trying to drive them in a positive direction is a wise strategy. It is also an important element of conflict management – being able to recognize, and respond to, the roots of more damaging levels of conflict.

Another common misunderstanding of conflict is that it is always a bad thing, that it is always harmful. Of course, it can be extremely harmful in a number of ways, but we should not allow the extent and severity of the damage it can do to distract us from the fact that there is also positive potential associated with conflict. Indeed, conflict can be helpful in terms of:

- *Innovation* People seeing situations differently, bringing different perspectives, points of view, priorities or expectations can be a rich source of creativity, fresh insights, breaking new ground and getting out of ruts and tramlines. Even where these differences are expressed angrily or confrontationally, the potential for innovation is still there. We can be missing opportunities for problem solving, empowerment and learning by failing to recognize the positive potential of conflict.

- *Freeing up* Similarly, conflicts can free up situations that have become stuck. It is very easy for people to get bogged down in a particular set of circumstances in which there appears to be no way forward. Conflict breaking out can disturb the status quo and thereby create opportunities for people to move forward (or even compel them to move forward). While this may be a tense and unpleasant experience, it can still have many positive benefits.

- *Earning respect* I have come across many situations where there has been a conflict between two or more people, sometimes a very severe and intense conflict, but the end result has been each party respecting the other. Standing your ground, fighting for what you believe in and not being prepared to abandon your principles can lead you into a lot of conflict, but it can also earn you a lot of respect and thereby credibility (as discussed in Section 3).

Conflict, then, is not a matter of hostility alone, nor is it necessarily a bad thing. Conflict is, in many ways, an inevitable part of social life – it is a reflection of difference and diversity. It is therefore something we need to learn to manage, rather than just try to avoid.

What can help us to manage conflict is an understanding of how it can play out at four different but connected levels, and that is what we are going to look at now.

The four levels

Conflict begins with difference. Of course, as the whole idea of valuing diversity has taught us, difference is a good thing; it would not do if everyone were the same, like peas in a pod. But, difference can also lead to problems if it is allowed to escalate. This is why it is helpful to think of conflict in terms of four levels, recognizing the harm that can be done if escalation from one level to the next occurs.

Everyday interactions

Conflict is commonly misunderstood as a breakdown of normality, whereas, at this level at least, it is part and parcel of everyday life. There will constantly be disagreements and differences of opinion, but for the most part we just take these in our stride. We use our basic social skills to manage such differences – for example, by politely disagreeing and remaining civil. We learn these skills from a very early age and generally have no difficulty in using them, although there will be exceptions. These can go in either direction. This is in the sense that, at one extreme, someone may disagree, but prefer not to air that disagreement (even though this may lead to problems further down the line), while, at the other extreme, someone may express their disagreement so strongly that it is considered impolite (and thereby creates tension).

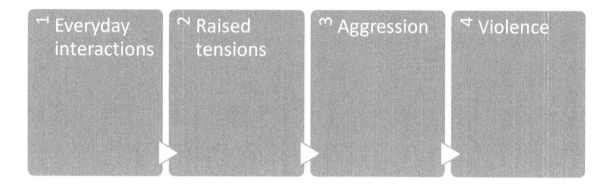

Raised tensions

In this latter case, we reach the level of raised tensions. This is where there is an 'edge' to the disagreement – for example, when tone of voice and/or body language indicate that the situation has gone beyond the first level of 'everyday interactions'. It is at this point that we should become aware of the danger of further escalation and start thinking of 'nipping things in the bud'. Of course, we would have to do this sensitively and tactfully, otherwise our intervention could, in itself, be what leads to the escalation.

At times it may be wise not to intervene at all, but that should be a judgement call based on carefully weighing up the situation (back to reflective practice again), rather than simply reacting in an unthinking, uncritical way. Many incidences of 'raised tensions' will fizzle out as quickly as they arose, but we need to be 'tuned in' to the situation, especially if further escalation has the potential to be very harmful.

Aggression

By the time conflict reaches this level, normal rules of social interaction have been abandoned. When someone is being aggressive, they are insisting on having their own way, even if this is at someone else's expense and at the expense of dispensing with everyday politeness. This can include a raised voice, threatening gestures, insulting comments and other tactics geared towards the aggressor having his or her own way.

In addition to this being problematic behaviour in its own right, there is a very real risk that the other party will respond in an equally aggressive way, leading to an escalation to the next level. But, this is not the only risk. The other party may become highly distressed, resulting in loss of trust and the breakdown of any basis for moving the situation forward constructively. They may also react not in a direct, confrontational way, but, rather, through sabotage – getting their own back in more subtle or indirect ways.

Violence

Aggression does not automatically lead to actual violence or a physical attack, but it can do, and, sadly, often does. Violence can range from fairly minor (pushing and shoving, for example) to murder. But, even at the minor level, it is something that needs to be avoided wherever possible, not least because of the emotional and interpersonal harm it can do. There is also, of course, the danger that violence begets violence, leading to a highly destructive spiral.

In view of the harm that can be done by escalation, a key element of conflict management is learning how to prevent such an escalation in the first place. Much of this depends on using our social work skills to intervene positively in difficult circumstances.

The RED approach

This is a tool or framework that I discuss in my *People Solutions Sourcebook* (Thompson, 2012a). RED spells out three steps to take:

- ➤ **R***ecognize the conflict* The tendency to equate conflict with hostility or aggression can mean that conflict in its earlier stages can easily be missed. Consequently, what can also be missed is opportunities to address any such conflicts before they escalate and do considerable harm.

  In addition, people involved in a conflict can easily mistake it for inappropriate behaviour on another person's part. For example, if Person A feels that Person B is 'being awkward' or 'being difficult', there is a high chance that Person B feels that Person A is being awkward or difficult too. In other words, what is actually a conflict between two people comes to be seen as a matter of individual misconduct. Again, conflict can be missed, and with it opportunities for positive intervention.

- ➤ **E***valuate it* Given that conflict is part of everyday life, it would be unrealistic for us to attempt to address every conflict we come across. Consequently, we have to be able to *evaluate* conflicts – that is, to weigh up how serious they are in terms of: (i) the likelihood of escalation; and (ii) the potential harm that could be done in the event of one or more escalations. In a sense, it is a form of risk assessment, and so we will return to this topic in Section 22.

- ➤ **D***eal with it* Ducking out of conflict can be a very unwise move, as unresolved conflicts can go on for a considerable time, causing a great deal of tension, ill feeling and problems. It is therefore essential that we do not allow our own anxiety or reluctance to prevent us from addressing conflict situations as skilfully and positively as we can.

Our starting point is to make good use of our existing social work skills (interpersonal skills especially). In addition, there are various conflict management tools or strategies that can be learned over time (see the *Guide to further learning* at the end of the manual).

Conclusion

Managing conflict can be challenging work at times, but the better informed we are, the more experienced we become, the more our confidence will grow and the more effective we will be. By contrast, if we shy away from conflict or just keep our fingers crossed that it will just go away, we are taking some significant risks, not least our credibility. If people notice that we are ducking out of conflict situations, they will have no confidence in us, and that loss of faith will significantly disempower us when it comes to trying to make a positive difference. It is therefore well worth the effort and personal investment to develop our conflict managements skills and confidence.

Managing Conflict Exercise

What do you see as the biggest challenges you face when it comes to managing conflict?
What do you need to work on to make you the most effective conflict manager you can be?

21. Loss, grief and trauma

A message that I have consistently tried to put across through my work is the vitally important idea that, wherever we go in social work, loss and grief issues are never far away. They may not always be recognized or acknowledged (indeed, they are often missed), but they will be there and they will be playing an important part in the situation in a significant proportion of cases. In this section, we will explore how problematic that can be and make the case for being constantly 'tuned in' to issues relating to loss and grief.

In addition, we are now seeing a growing awareness of the significance of trauma in people's lives – for example, in both the child abuse and mental health fields (and especially in the relationship between these two areas of practice). What this section will help to establish is that trauma is also a form of loss, and one that deserves our attention.

The grief paradox: prevalence and invisibility

Whenever we make an emotional investment ('cathexis', to use the technical term), in a person, a relationship or anything else, we run the risk of experiencing grief if or when we lose that person, relationship or whatever. In a very real sense, grief is the sense of emptiness or void that we feel when we experience a significant loss.

Conventionally there is a strong association between grief and bereavement. Indeed, for many people grief is understood narrowly as our response to death. However, this narrow view of loss and grief is misleading and unhelpful. This is because it means that other forms of loss (and thus sources of grief) are marginalized or even left out of the picture altogether.

This can be highly problematic, as we can have a distorted picture of the situations we are dealing with if we do not take account of the role grief is playing in the lives of the people concerned.

In reality, grief can arise in a wide range of loss situations, many of which we will encounter in social work:

Being abused ▲ family breakdown ▲ losing independence ▲ being 'in care' ▲ being the victim of crime ▲ becoming disabled ▲ losing self-respect through being discriminated against ▲ being homeless ▲ loss of role (as a carer, for example) ▲ loss of hope or aspiration ▲ loss of community ▲ loss of job

… and many more. The paradox, then, is that loss and grief are such common phenomena, and yet they are so often not recognized or dealt with.

An important concept in relation to this is that of 'disenfranchised grief' (Doka, 1989; 2017). This refers to grief that goes unacknowledged, resulting in the griever(s) not receiving support, thereby adding to a sense of isolation and vulnerability. There can be various forms of disenfranchised grief, not least the following:

- The *relationship* is not recognized – for example, when someone loses their secret lover and cannot grieve openly.

- The *loss* is not acknowledged or is stigmatized – for example, someone who takes their own life. Suicide is not as stigmatized as it once was, but a certain degree of disenfranchisement remains.

- The *griever* is not acknowledged – for example, people with learning disabilities where it is assumed that 'they won't understand', or older people who are assumed to 'get used to grief'.

To this list we can add losses that are not death related, as is so often the case in social work.

Clearly, then, there is a lot at stake if we neglect the significance of grief and fail to be sufficiently 'grief aware' in our practice.

>>> Moccasins moment <<<

Imagine that you have experienced a significant loss that is not connected with a death, but no one is recognizing that you are grieving. What impact might that have on the severity of your grief and your ability to cope with it?

Beyond stages

What complicates matters in relation to grief is that it is commonly assumed that people grieve in stages, even though there is little or no evidence to support this assumption. For one thing, people do not grieve in a straight line, so the term 'stages' was never a wise choice of terminology. For another, some of the 'stages' are not essential parts of the experience of grief. 'Bargaining' can occur, but does not always do so. Depression, another of the alleged stages, can often accompany grief, but will often not be present. Very significantly, depression and grief can appear superficially alike, but in reality they are very different. Grief is a painful, frightening and exhausting process of readjustment or healing following a major loss, and, despite the problems involved, is ultimately a positive and helpful process. Depression, by contrast, is when we are emotionally stuck or paralysed. Mistaking one for the other can mean that we are developing an inaccurate and misleading assessment that can lead to inappropriate helping responses on our part or the part of others.

The misleading idea that people grieve in stages became well established at one point and has proven extremely difficult to dispel. It has become prescriptive –

that is, many people who are grieving try to grieve according to the stages, as they feel that this is the proper thing to do. In reality, though, there is no set way to grieve, no fixed pattern. Different people grieve in different ways, partly due to differing social circumstances, partly due to personal characteristics, preferences and/or experiences, and partly due to how other people (including social workers) relate to them and their feelings. There is no 'one size fits all'.

If people don't grieve in stages, then what do they do and how should we respond? That is what we are going to turn our attention to now.

Responding to loss

There are various theories that help to cast light on the complexities involved in loss and grief (see Thompson, 2012b). One that can be particularly helpful is known as 'meaning reconstruction theory' developed by Robert Neimeyer and his colleagues (Neimeyer, 2001).

The basic idea behind this theory is that, when we experience a major loss, we not only lose the person or thing we are grieving for, we also lose what they mean to us, in the sense that what our life means can be irrevocably changed by the loss. Imagine, for example, that there is one person, and only one person, that you trust enough to confide in. Imagine also what the situation would be if you were to lose that person (through death, by falling out with them, because they have a major stroke or whatever other reason). This would involve losing not only that person from your life, but also your confidant, your opportunity to speak openly about your feelings and concerns. Up to now, confiding meant talking to your friend, but now confiding means something very different. It means that you will either have to find someone else to confide in or do without the benefits you gain from being able to confide in someone you trust. This aspect of meaning in your life has now changed.

This is an approach that has much to commend it at a theoretical level, but it is also a useful practice tool. What Neimeyer advocates is working with the grieving person(s) to help them develop new meanings. This is a form of 'narrative therapy' (Harms, 2018), a means of helping people create new meanings to enable them to get their lives on track again.

However, we should not automatically assume that anyone who is grieving necessarily needs grief counselling or psychotherapy. In reality, the vast majority of losses for the vast majority of people can be managed simply with everyday social supports. Professional input will only be needed in a minority of cases, so we need to make sure that we do not over-react. Recognizing that someone is grieving (and, if it is not obvious to them that they are grieving – which will be the case in many non-death-related loss situations – helping them to understand that this is what is happening) can be very beneficial and can help move things forward. But, it is important to note that, whatever we do to help, we cannot expect to take away the pain – however much we would like to. The pain is an intrinsic part of the process and, besides, trying to take the pain away can be seen to amount to failing to honour the loss and its significance.

Counselling, if required, can normally be accessed via voluntary organizations, such as Cruse if the situation warrants such an intervention (it is worth emphasizing again that we should not assume that grieving creates a need for counselling). But, as social workers, we should be looking more holistically at the situation: What issues, challenges, opportunities and risks have arisen because of the loss(es) experienced? What needs to be done to address the negatives and capitalize on the positives. Once again, it brings us back to reflective practice and the need for a carefully considered assessment.

This holistic approach should also mean that we take into consideration wider social factors, such as gender, race/ethnicity, poverty and so on. The dominant approach to issues relating to loss and grief has traditionally been an individualistic one that pays little or no attention to the social context. A social work perspective can help to counterbalance that narrowness of approach (Thompson and Cox, 2017).

People who have had a non-death-related loss may not realize they are grieving. They will no doubt be aware that something is wrong and that they are suffering, but not appreciate that grief is at the root of it. Sensitively helping them to realize they are grieving can be a very positive move forward.

Responding to trauma

Trauma comes from the Greek word for 'wound'. It is used in medical circles to refer to physical wounds, but it is also used to refer to psychological (or, more accurately, psychosocial) wounds. This refers to the way in which people's lives can be turned upside down because of abuse, being a victim of crime or other experiences that prove overwhelming. Without proper support, such traumatic experiences can have devastating effects on a long-term (even lifelong) basis.

We need to keep in mind (at least) two important points:

(i)   Trauma involves loss – often multiple and severe losses. Indeed, this is in large part why traumatic experiences are so overwhelming.

(ii)   Although we can contribute very positively to the lives of people who have been traumatized, we should not see ourselves as psychotherapists or assume that some form of counselling input is necessarily what is required. These are complex, multidimensional matters, and need to be understood – and responded to – as such. Once again a carefully considered assessment is needed.

For many years it was assumed that children who had been traumatized by abuse and subsequently removed to a place where they would be safe and be warmly and lovingly cared for, they would 'get over' their trauma. However, what we now realize much more fully is that this is not likely to happen, and a more sophisticated understanding of the complications involved is called for (Walsh  and Thompson, 2017). The focus now is on a structured and systematic process of trauma recovery. If, as is likely to be the case, you find yourself working with someone who has been traumatized (whether as a child or an adult), it will pay for you to develop your understanding by exploring the issues in more depth than we can realistically do in this manual (see the *Guide to further learning*).

Conclusion

We have to be realistic and recognize that, in this section, we have been able to only scratch the surface of some very complex and wide-ranging issues. But, it is to be hoped that it has been enough to demonstrate the need to be 'grief aware' and not fall into the trap of neglecting the significance of loss and grief in so many aspects of social work practice. It is also to be hoped that you can now understand trauma as a form of grief and appreciate the need for a carefully considered assessment, whether in relation to trauma or, indeed, any situation involving loss and grief.

Loss, Grief and Trauma Exercise

What detrimental effect do you think it might have if someone's grief is not recognized and they are not offered the support they need? What consequences could it lead to for them and for you as a social worker?

22. Risk and decision making

In social work practice we are constantly making decisions, whether formally or informally, constantly deciding what to do and what not to do. At every step along the way, we are engaging with risk. Indeed, there is no such thing as a risk-free zone in social work. We therefore need to be well informed about risk issues and confident enough to deal with them in a balanced way without under- or over-reacting.

Our focus in this section, then, is on clarifying the significance of risk, appreciating the need for a balanced approach, exploring what is involved in risk assessment and risk management.

Balancing risk

This is a vitally important concept. If we are blasé about risk and fail to consider the dangers involved in a given situation, we will be behaving irresponsibly and will rightly be open to censure for a lack of professionalism. However, there is also a danger of getting it wrong by going to the opposite extreme, that of being 'risk averse'. This refers to over-reacting in relation to risk, being overly cautious and thereby relying on a distorted picture of the risks involved. We therefore need to draw on reflective practice again to weigh up carefully the issues involved – rather than rely on an anxiety-driven risk-averse approach that has the potential to be highly problematic.

Consider the following aspects of risk:

➤ *New risks for old* Removing or reducing one set of risks will introduce a new set of risks. For example, older people struggling to cope in the community and leaving their home to enter residential care will be in a less risky situation

212

compared with fending for themselves alone in the community, but residential care is not, of course, without its risks (consider the potential emotional devastation of having to give up one's home and independence). Similarly, there are many cases on record of children being removed from abusive families and then subsequently being further abused in foster care or residential care. It is therefore essential, when focusing on removing or reducing risks, that we also balance these out with any possible risks that are being introduced in doing so. Unfortunately, in my work as an expert witness and independent investigator, I have come across many cases where such a balance was not considered and the result was highly detrimental. It would be very naïve to think that we can create a risk-free situation.

➢ *Risks empower* Risks bring danger and potential harm, which is why, of course, in our decision making, we place a great deal of emphasis on them. However, we would be adopting a highly unbalanced picture of risk if we were to not also recognize the positive side of risk. Consider, for example, the things you really enjoy doing. How would you feel if you were prevented from doing these things because of the risks involved? What would be the point of sport if there were no risks involved? If a risk-free life were even possible, it would be an incredibly dispiriting one. Risk can be empowering, in the sense that we need to take risks in order to gain greater control over our lives. A risk-averse approach is therefore disempowering and thus oppressive.

➢ *Risk and rights* Another 'side effect' of an unbalanced risk-averse approach is that, if we are not careful, we can deny people their rights. For example, an older person who has mental capacity has the right to live in the community, even at a high level of risk, if they so choose. Consequently, putting them under undue pressure to leave the community can amount to a denial of rights, making us part of the problem, rather than part of the solution.

It should be clear, then, that we need to aim for a balanced approach to risk at all times. It is essential that we do not allow anxiety (our own or other people's) to drive us in the direction of an unbalanced risk-averse approach.

Assessing risk

Risk is a complex matter, and so if we are to be able to handle it effectively and incorporate it into our decision-making processes, then we need a fairly sophisticated understanding of risk and associated matters and a helpful way of assessing risk.

There are various risk assessment tools available, but, whatever tool or tools we choose to use, we need to be very clear that there is no foolproof 'scientific' way of assessing risk that guarantees that we will get it right every time. This is, of course, because risk assessment is in itself a risky business. We are back to the idea that there is no such thing as a risk-free zone.

>>> Moccasins moment <<<

Imagine someone is trying to stop you doing things that are important to you, perhaps even part of your identity, because they disapprove of the level of risk involved. Even if they were doing this 'for your own good', would you see their actions as supportive or oppressive?

Assessing risk involves an element of prediction or forecasting – trying to anticipate what will happen and what effects it might have. So, inevitably, we will get it wrong sometimes. Consequently, what we need to aim for is:

(i)   Getting it right as often as possible by making sure that our analysis has been sufficiently thorough (no skimping), wide ranging (not too narrow in its focus) and reflective (based on careful consideration, not driven by anxiety).

(ii)   Making sure that the rationale for our decision making is properly documented for purposes of: (a) professional accountability; and (b) future learning.

Once again it is a matter of balance. If we are searching for some sort of holy grail of a guaranteed way of assessing risk, we are wasting our time and energy. However, if we go to the other extreme and think that we can just guess about risks or rely on our 'intuition', we are failing to do the best risk assessment possible. As I mentioned earlier, there are tools available that can be helpful if used as part of reflective practice, and so we are not having to simply rely on uninformed predictions. However, we should be wary of the simplistic idea that ticking some boxes on a risk assessment form is sufficient in itself. It is the professionally well-informed analysis that goes with the tool that can make all the difference.

We should also not forget that risk assessment can and should be done in partnership. This involves, where feasible, taking on board the perspective, views and experience of the person(s) concerned, as well as including the views and understanding of family members, other professionals and potentially any other interested parties.

Risk assessment is a complex and tricky business. It needs careful consideration and a calm, balanced approach. In particular, it needs to be based on reflective practice, and not on anxiety or defensiveness.

Managing risk

There are two main types of decision in social work. There are formal decisions that are made by courts, statutory reviews, tribunals, resource allocation panels and so on. There are also informal decisions taken on a day-to-day basis (Shall I visit today or leave it until tomorrow?). Both types of decision involve risk and, ideally, should involve a good understanding of the risk issues involved. Of course, we cannot carry out a formal, detailed risk assessment every time we are deciding whether today or tomorrow is the better day to make that visit – but risk should none the less be part of the consideration. Indeed, risk can be understood as part of any decision-making process.

Decision making, whether formal or informal, involves identifying possible courses of action and choosing which is the most appropriate in the circumstances. So, once again, there is an element of prediction or forecasting. We cannot guarantee that we have made the decision that will produce the best results, but we will – or at least, should – have done the best we can to arrive at the optimal decision by weighing up the relevant factors and circumstances carefully.

Risk management is therefore part of decision making, but decision making is also part of risk management, in the sense that, once we are aware of significant risk factors, we need to be deciding on a day-to-day basis how best to manage the situation, how best we can play a positive role in keeping people safe without stifling them or denying them their rights. The idea that a risk assessment is something that is completed and then forgotten, is a very dangerous and destructive idea (although one I have come across on more than a few occasions).

Again, it is important to remember that risk is an issue (or set of issues) that needs to be managed in partnership, not in isolation. This is why, for example, safeguarding conferences are multidisciplinary events. We have to avoid allowing ourselves to be pushed (or push ourselves) into a situation where we feel isolated and that the burden of risk management is ours alone. Leaving it to one person is not the best way to manage complex, tricky situations, and nor is it a positive thing to do in terms of self-care and stress avoidance. There is also, in such circumstances, a greater likelihood that you will allow anxiety to be a strong influence and that, in turn, makes it more likely that the client's voice will not be heard – they can become the 'object of concern', rather than a key, active partner in the undertaking.

What is also important is to remember to see risk assessment issues as part of the wider assessment – that is, the wider picture of what the problems and needs are; what the strategies for addressing those problems and needs are; what strengths and resilience factors there are in the situation; and what can be done to capitalize on them. In other words, it is essential that we do not make the mistake of allowing the risk issues to become the be all and end all of our intervention. At times, some practitioners have told me that they have come to feel that their job is just about managing risk. I have always responded by saying they have to make sure that they do not lose sight of the wider picture and what  their role is (see Sections 2 and 23). Risk is an important part of the picture, but it is not the whole picture – we must not allow it to become the cuckoo in the nest.

 Anxiety about risk is, in my experience, the biggest obstacle to managing risk effectively. It is therefore essential that we do not allow anxiety to stand in the way of assessing and managing risk.

Conclusion

We are constantly making decisions in social work, and risk factors are a central part of the processes involved. While it is understandable that this area of our practice can be quite daunting, what is needed is a calm, reflective, balanced approach, one that does not allow anxiety or defensiveness cloud our judgement and lead us into being risk averse. To put it paradoxically, playing it safe is dangerous. That is, if we are over-cautious we will actually create more problems than we solve, and potentially do a great deal of harm.

Risk and Decision Making Exercise

What factors are likely to lead social workers and other professionals to be risk averse? What can be done to stop this happening or to keep their effects to a minimum? What might the costs be if we allow a risk-averse approach to flourish?

23. Focusing on outcomes

Social work is complex, multidimensional and demanding. We can have demands made on us from all angles and be subject to conflicting expectations from various parties, and all this in a context that can change significantly at any moment. This is partly why I have long argued that a key social work skill is the ability to manage complexity.

One of the consequences of all this complexity and the confusion it can engender is that practitioners can, at times, get so embroiled in a situation that they cannot see the wood for the trees – that is, they lose the plot, they lose track of their role and what they are trying to achieve. We touched on this point in Section 2, but now I want to revisit it and explore it in more depth. This is because losing our way or losing our focus can mean that a lot of time, effort and scarce resources can be wasted, people we are trying to help or support can become confused and alienated and lose out in various other ways also. Staying focused is therefore essential, and that is precisely what this section is about. We explore the significance of clear outcomes and present the idea of 'systematic practice' as a tool for keeping our practice clear and focused.

What is an outcome?

An outcome is the desired end result. It is what we are working towards. In other words, it is what we are trying to achieve.
For example, if we are working in a situation in which one or more people are facing an unacceptably high level of risk (of abuse, for instance), then a key outcome that we would be working towards would be the reduction of that risk to an acceptable level.

What it comes down to is, as discussed earlier, being clear about why we are involved with this person, family or group. Social work time is a scarce resource, and so it is important that it is not wasted. We therefore have to have a *purpose*, a reason for being involved in people's lives. Outcome-focused practice is based on the idea that we must be very clear what that purpose is, what the reason is for investing time and energy in a particular situation. If we are not clear, we can not only waste time and resources, but also create problems (for example, by generating confusion that gets in the way of progress).

We should therefore: (i) think of outcomes as the goals or objectives we are aiming for; and (ii) make sure that, however, complex, confusing, conflicted and changing a situation may be, we must not lose sight of what outcomes we are working towards.

Why are outcomes important?

There are four main reasons why outcomes are not only important, but actually essential to good practice. These are:

➢ *Clarity* If it is not clear what we are trying to achieve, it will not be clear what our role is, and that, of course will generate confusion and some degree of insecurity. If, by contrast, we have explicit, agreed outcomes that we are working towards, there can be much more clarity and a much firmer basis to work from.

➢ *Motivation* Having clear, agreed goals can also be a significant source of motivation for all concerned (including the social worker). If we are not clear where we are trying to get to or how we are going to get there, this fuzziness is more likely to demotivate than to motivate. If, however, we have managed to establish, through the process of assessment, some degree of clarity about what outcomes we are working towards and what we need to do to achieve them, we have a much better foundation for motivation.

➤ *Time and workload management* If we are practising in a way that is unfocused, a lot of time and energy can be wasted. Clarity about outcomes and remaining focused on them can therefore help to ensure that we are more effective in making best use of the limited time we have available to us. Also, I have come across a number of situations in which the outcomes had been achieved, but the social worker had remained involved unnecessarily, risking the creation of dependency. Congratulating people that they no longer need our help is a much wiser option than staying involved after we have achieved what we set out to. We can't have it both ways; we can't complain that we have too much to do, while also wasting time doing things that are no longer necessary because we lost sight of the outcomes we were working towards.

>>> Moccasins moment <<<

How motivated would you be if a professional were visiting you and/or your family, but they were not making it clear why they were there or what the object of the exercise was? How might that contrast with having clear agreed goals to work towards?

➤ *Working in partnership* As we have noted, social work needs to be carried out in partnership – it is something we do *with* people, not to or for them. Negotiating clear outcomes gives us a firm basis for developing such a partnership. We can work *together* if we know what we are working *towards*, but if we lack clarity about outcomes, there is likely to be confusion that can soon result in suspicion and resistance. We cannot expect people (the people we serve or fellow professionals) to trust us if it is not clear where we are trying to get to, and without that trust partnership is going to be more or less impossible. By contrast, involving people in a process of identifying needs, problems, strengths and resilience factors and thereby establishing what needs to change will generate not only clear outcomes, but also the trust and commitment needed to move forward positively.

221

There is much more that could be said about why outcomes are important, but what we have covered here should be more than enough to establish that it would be very unwise to settle for forms of practice that are not driven by clarity about purpose and outcomes.

Systematic practice

One well-established tool for facilitating outcome-focused practice is systematic practice (Thompson, 2015a; 2015b). This involves three key questions that we need to be able to answer to make sure that we are not losing sight of outcomes:

1. *What are you trying to achieve?*

This is where we need to explicitly identify the outcome (or set of outcomes) we need to work towards. It should arise from the assessment process that involves gathering information to form a picture of the situation that we are dealing with. It should be carried out in partnership of course. Outcomes are normally not things we should be seeking to impose on people, but, rather, the result of negotiation. The exception is situations where there may be statutory or other legitimate reasons why we have to exercise authority in ways that could involve insisting on certain outcomes being included in our assessment – for example, as a result of a court order or a decision made at a child protection case conference. However, we should make sure that any such imposing is a last resort. This is because imposed change is generally the least successful change, so we should aim to secure agreement wherever possible.

What are you trying to achieve?

How are you going to achieve it?

How will you know when you have achieved it?

2. *How are you going to achieve it?*

This question is about planning. It is asking you what your plan is, what steps you need to take to achieve the outcomes identified. Again, this needs to be done in partnership. It involves clarifying what is likely to bring about the changes needed.

It is important to be clear here that this may involve providing or commissioning services, but we should not make the mistake of adopting a consumerist approach in assuming that service provision is the primary means of making progress (we shall return to the problems of consumerism in Section 26). This second question presents us with an opportunity to use reflective practice to be creative and imaginative in exploring ways of moving forward positively.

3. *How will you know when you have achieved it?*

Unfortunately, this is a question that is often forgotten about, even though it is very important. What makes it so important is that it helps to make sure that we have answered the first two questions properly. Basically, this question is asking us what success will look like. If we are too vague or general in answering either or both of the first two questions, we will struggle to be able to answer this third question. It therefore disciplines us in answering the questions in a very specific and focused way. As social workers we are involved in helping, supporting, protecting and empowering people, but using these terms in a very broad, generalized way is not helpful:

- Helping to achieve what precisely?
- Supporting people in achieving what specific outcome?
- Protecting them from what exactly?
- Empowering people in what specific way for what specific purpose?

Having a fairly clear and precise vision of what you actually mean – in specific terms – by success will stand you in good stead. Knowing what success looks like will enable you to determine when you have completed what you set out to do and then decide whether your involvement comes to an end or a new set of outcomes needs to be addressed.

Conclusion

Losing the plot, becoming unfocused and drifting is an easy mistake to make in the complex, confusing and demanding world of social work. However, it is a very costly mistake and one that we would do well to avoid. Sadly, it is a common mistake, one that I have come across time and time again. I have had many conversations with social workers (in my capacity as a manager, trainer,

 consultant, investigator or expert witness) where it has quickly become apparent to me that they either did not clarify outcomes at the beginning of their involvement, or somewhere along the line they had lost sight of those outcomes.

Part of the problem is that some practitioners seem to feel that just generally trying to be helpful in whatever ways they can is a clear enough focus for their work. As we shall see in Section 26, this 'general helper' model of social work is highly problematic. It is no substitute for having a systematic approach with clear outcomes to work towards, a clear plan for moving forward and clarity about what success will look like (so that you know when you have arrived at your destination).

Finally, it is important to emphasize that being systematic and outcome focused does not mean being rigid. Circumstances will change, of course, so we may need to recognize that desired outcomes have changed or the means of achieving them may need to change (some doors close, others open). But, however much we may need to rethink and renegotiate our answers to the three key questions, the need to keep those questions in mind remains undiminished.

If we lose our focus, we lose our way, we lose our credibility, we lose trust and we therefore lose our ability to make a positive difference – we become ineffective. Systematic, outcome-focused practice is therefore not a particular tool or technique we should use in some circumstances, but not others – it is a fundamental dimension of good practice. Our reflective practice therefore needs to include continually reflecting on outcomes and how we are planning on achieving them.

Many of the people who have attended training courses I have run on outcome-focused practice have taken my advice of having some sort of reminder of the three key questions available to them – on a card, for example, Many of them have subsequently told me that they found this very helpful.

Focusing on Outcomes Exercise

What detrimental effects could it have if you were to lose sight of outcomes and practise in an unfocused way? What impact would it have on: (i) the people you are trying to help; (ii) other professionals involved in the case; and (iii) your own credibility as a worker?

24. Handling dilemmas and tensions

'Damned if you do, damned if you don't' is a phrase commonly associated with social work, and it does often seem as though we can't win. Dilemmas and tensions are part of life and therefore largely unavoidable, but in social work we tend to get more than our fair share of them. It can make life difficult at times, but it can also make it interesting, challenging in a rewarding way and satisfying.

In this section we explore some of those common dilemmas and tensions and consider their significance. We begin by clarifying what we mean by a dilemma.

What is a dilemma?

A dilemma is a situation in which we have to choose between two or more options, each of which is potentially problematic. It will often involve having to decide which is the lesser of two evils. Such situations present a challenge to our decision-making skills and once again reinforce the importance of reflective practice – trying to resolve a dilemma without engaging our critical analysis skills and drawing on our value base can create immense difficulties.

Of course, there are many such dilemmas associated with social work, not least the following:

> *Care vs control* One of the criticisms of some groups outside of social work is that it is just a subtle form of social control, just a means of keeping people in line and preventing revolutionary uprisings. While it has to be recognized that there is a potential for this to happen, seeing this as the primary basis of social work is to demonstrate a lack of understanding of the subtleties involved, an oversimplification of a highly complex social phenomenon. However, it would

be naïve not to recognize that there are elements of social control within social work. But, this is not necessarily a bad thing. For example, protecting children or vulnerable adults from abuse may contain elements of controlling the perpetrators. Similarly, helping young offenders to steer clear of crime may at times involve elements of control. The key issues are whether the elements of control are: (i) part of an ethos of caring, not just controlling for its own sake; and (ii) kept to a minimum and used only where necessary.

*** KEY POINT ***

We need to be very wary of simplistically seeing care and control as polar opposites. They are interwoven in subtle and complex ways and therefore need to be considered carefully.

> *Risk vs rights* As we noted in Section 22 there can be tensions between risks and rights. Focusing narrowly on risks can result in a person's rights being infringed, while focusing narrowly on rights can mean that a person is not aware of the risks they are being exposed to, and are therefore not in a position to make informed choices about those risks and their potential consequences. The tension between rights and risk is therefore one that we need to be aware of and not allow a defensive, risk-averse approach to drive us in the direction of prioritizing risk over rights. This is because infringing someone's rights is not only ethically and professionally (and possibly legally) unacceptable, it is also potentially counterproductive, as it will introduce a new set of risks as well as destroying or at least undermining trust.

> *Authority vs empowerment* Helping people to gain greater control over their lives and circumstances is what empowerment is all about, but how can that be squared with social workers exercising authority at times? It needs to be remembered that authority is, by definition, the use of *legitimate* power – power that is being used for positive purposes. Indeed, a key element of social work empowerment is that we use *our* power to help others develop and make use of *their* power. In technical terms, it is power *with*, rather than power *over*

(Thompson, 2007). We should therefore not fail to exercise our authority where necessary for fear of standing in the way of empowerment. We should at all times be using whatever power we have ethically and in an informed way. Using power inappropriately or when we do not need to is unethical, but so too is failing to use our power appropriately when the situation demands it. This is all part of being a professional (see Section 8).

➢ *Family care vs substitute care* The value of home and family is well established in social work and wider society. Consequently, much of social work intervention is geared towards keeping people within their own home and thus within their own community. However, there will be times when staying at home is either not feasible (due to it not being possible for care needs to be met there, for example) or not desirable (abuse within the family being the most common reason).

Sometimes it is crystal clear that a child or vulnerable adult needs to leave their home, but very often it will be a difficult judgement call that involves weighing up all the pros and cons in order to arrive at a balanced decision. This needs to be done in partnership, of course, but there will be times when that is not possible (for example, where an abused child wants to stay at home, but it has been deemed that it is not safe for them to do so). Where it is necessary to find substitute care (foster care or residential care, for example), this needs to be handled very sensitively, of course, with due regard to the wishes and feelings of the individuals concerned. Where possible, the transition needs to be gradual, allowing the individual concerned to make the necessary adjustments. Returning to the theme of Section 21, we also need to be tuned in to the grief issues involved.

➢ *Needs vs wants* There can sometimes be a tension between what people want and what they need. This can work in two directions. First, they may not want what they need (as in the example I mentioned a moment ago of an abused child who needs to be removed from home for their own safety, but does not want to be). This may at times form the basis of statutory intervention (through a court order, for example) where the severity of the situation requires this. Second, there can be times when what people want is not what they need – for example, when someone does not meet the eligibility criteria for a particular service or where there is a more appropriate way of meeting their needs. Such situations will then need further negotiation, as we cannot give people a service they want but don't need.

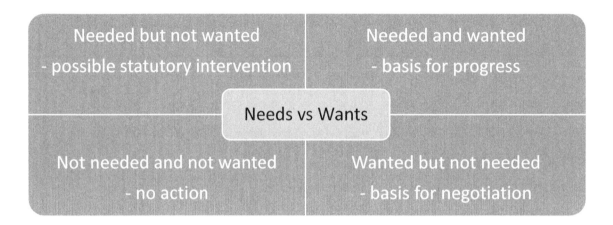

When what they want and what they need coincide, we have a basis for progress. In those circumstances where there is something they neither want nor need, we need to take no further action. The grid above can help us get a clear picture of the different combinations and what they entail.

> *Needs vs budgets* Social work, like other areas of social policy, is faced with the challenge of having finite resources due to budget limitations, but potentially infinite demand. Even if the budget were to be double or trebled, there is still the potential for demand to exceed supply. Consequently, we cannot escape the problem of managing limited resources. This is a very difficult area of practice and often one that creates a lot of frustration for practitioners and managers. On the one hand, we need to be realistic and recognize that there will be budget limitations, but, on the other hand, we have to recognize our duty to meet people's needs as far as we possibly can. One way of managing this is to make sure that we are not engaging in consumerist practices (that is, focusing exclusively or primarily on service provision, rather than more creatively exploring ways of meetings people's

needs and addressing their problems and challenges – see Section 26). Consumerism places unrealistic pressures on available resources and, if we are not careful, can reduce professional practice to an administrative process of simply gatekeeping scarce resources (rather than using reflective practice to explore how we can make the best use of those limited resources).

This is by no means a comprehensive list of dilemmas and tensions – far from it – but it does demonstrate just how much of an issue such dilemmas and tensions are in social work. What we have covered should therefore help us to realize how prepared we need to be for managing such challenges.

We will never be able to escape these matters, but we can learn how to manage them as in intrinsic part of social work. It is therefore to the question of *managing* dilemmas and tensions that we now turn.

Managing dilemmas and tensions

Specific instances of dilemmas and tensions can be resolved as and when they arise. However, what we have to recognize is that the dilemmas themselves cannot be resolved – they are ever-present. For example, we can resolve an instance of a tension between authority and empowerment in the way we handle the particular case circumstances at the time. But, however many times we do this, the tension between authority and empowerment will always be there.

It is for this reason that I am talking about *managing* dilemmas, rather than resolving them. Given the complexity of the issues involved, it should not come as a surprise to you to learn that there are no simple, formula responses – once again it is a matter of carefully considered and well-informed reflective practice.

Some key aspects of this will be:

- *Keeping the channels of communication open* We are not on our own in managing the dilemmas and tensions, so we need to make sure that other key players are aware of what the issues are and what needs to be considered. This is an important part of working in partnership.

Don't make the mistake of assuming that you are all alone in this. The challenges of various dilemmas and tensions will generally affect other people who may want to have a say or may be able to help cast light on how best to proceed. Don't isolate yourself.

- *Acting in good faith* This includes not giving in to risk-averse pressures, not being seduced by power, not losing sight of why we are involved with the person(s) concerned. In other words, we need to make sure that we hold on to our professionalism in what can be challenging times where shortcuts can sometimes be appealing (but dangerous).

- *Using our analytical skills* As I have emphasized, making sense of complex situations is a basic part of social work, and so we need to draw on the analytical skills that are part and parcel of managing complexity. Unfortunately, what can easily happen is that the tensions involved can make us anxious, which in turn makes us rush in order to get out of the situation as quickly as possible. That rushing then involves bypassing the use of our all-important analytical skills.

- *Not losing sight of our values* It is understandable – but not acceptable – that, at certain times of pressure and tension, we may be tempted to act in ways that are not consistent with our values. Indeed, our values can be an invaluable guide to decision making in such difficult circumstances, so the irony is that we may be letting go of or values precisely at one of the time when they can be of most benefit to us.

As I have emphasized, social work cannot be done effectively in a formulaic way – it is a creative enterprise, not an exercise in painting by numbers. We will constantly be faced with new challenges and we will need to use our reflective practice skills to rise to those challenges and make sense of the complexities involved.

Conclusion

I began this section by making the point that life itself is full of dilemmas and tensions, but social work especially so. One of the implications of this is that each of us already had a background in managing dilemmas and tensions before we even came into social work. So, in a sense, what is needed is a process of taking those basic skills to a more advanced level. We can begin to do this by asking ourselves what we have done in  our personal lives that has been successful in managing dilemmas. What strategies have worked well for us?

Equally, we can ask ourselves what mistakes or miscalculations we have made and, importantly, what lessons we have learned from these. The scope for learning from our own experience is once again quite significant.

Finding dilemmas and tensions challenging is not something that should concern or disconcert us. Indeed, it is all part of the great adventure of social work and, as such, can be a source of great satisfaction, motivation and pride.

Handling Dilemmas Exercise

What would you see as the greatest dilemma or tension facing you in your social work career? What is the source of that tension and what might you be able to do about it? Who would be the best person to support you in exploring these important issues?

25. Handling criticism

Some vocations are held in high regard by society, and so praise is often the starting point. Nurses – perceived as angels – are a prime example. I am in no way questioning the value and quality of what nurses do, but I am making the important point that positive perceptions are the starting point – the goodwill is theirs to lose for nurses. Other professions are not so fortunate. For example, without traffic wardens, city streets could be chaotic and even more problematic in terms of traffic flow than they already are. Traffic wardens therefore do an important and socially valuable job, despite the fact that they are generally held in very low regard by the general public. Praise and a positive response are things traffic wardens have to earn, against the odds, rather than their starting point.

Unfortunately, in these terms, social workers have more in common with traffic wardens than with nurses: doing a socially important and valuable job, but not necessarily being perceived as such by society at large. Consequently, as social workers, we can find that we are often exposed to unfair criticism, sometimes very harsh and punitive criticism. This is not to say that criticism is always misdirected, as, of course, all groups of people will get things wrong from time to time and/or allow their practice to fall below an acceptable standard. Rather, it is a case of recognizing that people who do not understand or value social work  (including many journalists and large sectors of the general public) will often put forward criticisms that do not fit with the facts of the situation.

Such unfair criticisms can be disheartening, demotivating and, at times, infuriating. This can then be problematic for us as social workers and for the people we serve. It is therefore important to be aware of the potential adverse effects of criticism and try to make sure that we keep any such negative effects to a minimum. That is precisely what this section is all about.

Doing society's dirty work

One of the points I make in my *Understanding Social Work* book is that part of the reason there is a lot of (largely unjustified) negativity towards social work and social workers is that much of what we do involves, as I put it: 'doing society's dirty work'. For example, many people are not aware (and do not want to accept) that child abuse is so widespread; they do not want to face up to the fact that there are so many individuals and families wrestling with abuse, discrimination, oppression, exploitation, poverty, deprivation, homelessness, family breakdown, trauma, mental health problems, and so on, and various combination of these challenges.

The lack of awareness is compounded by the dominant ideology that presents so many social problems as the failings of individual, rather than complex psychosocial issues that have their roots in the social order and in social policies. For example, poverty is widely understood as being due to a lack of moral fibre and laziness; homelessness as a 'lifestyle' choice; and mental health problems as simply 'diseases of the mind', with no acknowledgement of the highly significant role of social factors in generating mental distress.

Don't lose sight of your 'privileged' position, in the sense of having a much better overview of society and its problems than the vast majority of people will have. We cannot expect others to have the insights we have without having had our training and experience.

Consequently, the pressures on social workers tend not to be fully recognized, nor are the complexity and demanding nature of the work. For example, the simplistic general public understanding of social work is likely to be based on the idea that failures on the part of social workers to recognize abuse are due to incompetence because they failed to spot the 'symptoms'. In reality, of course, it is commonly the case that abuse occurs without any visible or recognizable indicators being apparent. In addition, there are very few indicators of abuse that could not have arisen for reasons other than abuse – bruising could be a sign of physical abuse, but there could be many other reasons why a bruise was sustained.

In such situations, what social workers are dealing with are highly complex, sensitive matters where there is rarely a clear-cut path to follow. Undoubtedly, if the general public were more fully aware of what is involved in social work (and not just in abuse-related situations), there would be much less unfair criticism and much more appreciation and praise.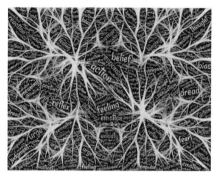

However, even with a greater level of understanding and awareness, it is still likely that we would receive some degree of unfair criticism, as the complex dynamics that go on in social work cases cannot be easily explained. Furthermore, the part played by the media in relation to social work is generally not a positive one. It is therefore to that topic that we now turn.

Understanding the media

We need to remember that the media are, for the most part, profit-making businesses and not educational institutions. Their primary goal, with few exceptions, is to make as much profit as they can. We should therefore not be naïve enough to think that they will prioritize in any way educating the public about any particular topic, and that includes social work.

Good news stories about social work successes will not sell newspapers or increase viewing or listening figures in the same way that sensationalized scandals about alleged incompetence will do, especially in the populist tabloids (which sadly tend to be the best-selling newspapers). There will therefore always be a bias towards the negative in terms of social work reporting, and some media outlets will not worry about accuracy or fairness (see Ray Jones's excellent book on the Baby Peter case for a helpful discussion of this – Jones, 2014).

Similarly, soap operas and dramas will not necessarily let accuracy stand in the way of what is perceived as good drama, so we should not be surprised when social work gets less than fair treatment in the media. However, we should not feel that we are being singled out in this regard. Think about how far removed hospital dramas are from the real-life world of a hospital setting or how so many police dramas bear no resemblance to actual police work. This is a question of media distortion in general and not just a social work concern.

 What is worrying and potentially problematic about this biased and misleading representation is that it can have a negative influence on members of the general public. Any citizens we work with may start from a position of mistrust because of the negative perception of social workers that has been fed by the media. This makes it all the more important that we are able to:

- *Set out our stall* As discussed in Section 6, it is important that, as a basis for working in partnership, we are able to 'set out our stall' effectively – that is, to make it clear what we do and what we don't do. Clearing up media misrepresentations can be part of this. We can make it clear what the reality of our role is and, if necessary, explicitly state that this can be very different from what the media have led people to believe.

- *Make the all-important human connection* As discussed in Section 13, to be as effective as possible, we need to build trust, and to build trust we need to be skilful and confident in 'connecting' with people, in building a positive rapport fairly quickly. Doing this effectively will very quickly dispel any negative expectations in the majority of cases. The more experienced we become at this, the more skilful we can become, and the more skilful we are, the less of a problem media distortion will be.

Complaints

Another potential source of criticism is the complaints procedure. As part of a commitment to empowerment, organizations that employ social workers will generally encourage anyone who is not happy with the help they are receiving to raise it as an issue. This will often be done through a formal complaints procedure. That people have easy opportunities to air their concerns is a positive and worthwhile thing. However, the downside is that having a complaint made against you is not a pleasant experience and can be very disheartening.

Complaints will often come from the needs vs wants dilemma we discussed in Section 24. That is, someone who is being denied what they want, but don't necessarily need, may feel hard done by and see making a complaint as a means of gaining redress.

Conflicts about any aspect of the situation can also lead to complaints, and this can generally be a good, if less than ideal, way of addressing such conflicts.

Misunderstandings about what a social worker can and cannot do will also often be a source of complaints, which once again emphasizes the importance of setting out our stall and developing positive forms of partnership working. Trying to make sure that our expectations and other people's match up is an essential basis for effective partnership (and a good way of avoiding complaints).

Of course, complaints can also arise because people have a genuine grievance, because we, or our organization have let them down in some way. In such circumstances, we are given an opportunity to: (i) address any concerns positively and constructively and thereby enable progress to be made; and (ii) learn from the experience with a view to preventing such problems arising in future.

Don't take it personally!

What should be clear from the discussion so far is that criticism is structurally built in to contemporary social work and probably always will be. It is therefore essential that we do not take these matters personally – they are largely inherent in the nature of the work we do.

Of course, there may well be times when we have made a mistake or let ourselves down in some way, but these can be excellent opportunities to learn and develop. If we expect to get it right 100% of the time, we are setting ourselves up to fail and, in effect, giving ourselves false expectations that we cannot live up to.

 It is essential from a self-care point of view that we do not take criticisms personally. Social work can be emotionally demanding enough without unnecessarily adding a further layer of emotional challenge.

Traffic wardens will get criticised for doing a socially important job (regardless of how well or appropriately they do it), tax inspectors will get criticised, despite the fact that public services would not be possible without taxation, and social workers will get criticised for the various reasons outlined here. It is not a reflection of the quality or otherwise or commitment of any single social worker.

Conclusion

Being criticised is not a pleasant or welcome experience, but it is one that 'goes with the territory' to a certain extent in social work. What we need, then, is a balanced approach. On the one hand, we should not let it get under our skin or take it personally (we need to understand it more holistically as part of a much bigger and more complex picture), while, on the other hand, doing everything we reasonably can to limit the amount and severity of criticism. This would include:

(i) at a personal level, making sure that we set out our stall to avoid misunderstandings or unrealistic expectations and remain professional in all our actions; and (ii) at a collective level, work with our professional organizations to promote more positive images of social work and to challenge media distortions and misrepresentations.

Achieving such a balance is not necessarily an easy thing to do, but it is important enough to warrant our persistent and consistent commitment to doing the best we can to bring about that balance.

Handling Criticism Exercise

What do you feel could be done to better publicize social work's successes and the value of what the profession brings in making our society a more humane one?

26. Pitfalls to avoid

All jobs will have potential pitfalls associated with them, but, given the broad range of social work issues, the complexity of the issues involved and the sensitive nature of much of the work, it is understandable that social work will have more than its fair share of pitfalls. It would be well beyond the scope of this manual to try and cover all of them. Consequently, what I am going to do is focus on different *types* of pitfall that can arise, as this should provide a foundation of knowledge on which to build.

But, before we do that, it is important to note that: (i) pitfalls lead to mistakes and can result in failure; and (ii) such mistakes and failures are an inevitable part of social work. In other words, however primed we are to be aware of pitfalls (forewarned is forearmed)

or however conscientious we are, there will be occasional mistakes and some degree of failure. Anyone coming into social work who expects a one hundred per cent success rate is heading for a major disappointment. More realistically, it is a matter of trying to make sure that we do the best we can in difficult circumstances. This involves doing the best we can to avoid pitfalls and mistakes by being entirely professional at all times – but being professional and being successful are not the same thing, of course.

This echoes what we will encounter with the people we serve. However hard they try to address their problems, however much support they receive from others, there is no guarantee of success. Again, it is a matter of doing the best we can in difficult circumstances, but accepting that some degree of failure will be part of that.

Types of pitfall

We are going to explore four different types of pitfall, those that relate to thoughts, feelings, actions and values – four fundamental aspects of human experience in general and social work in particular. The categories are not mutually exclusive and some pitfalls will have characteristic of more than one of the four types. However, this simple framework should be helpful in giving you a picture of how pitfalls can arise and therefore how you can be reasonably well equipped to deal with them or, ideally, prevent them.

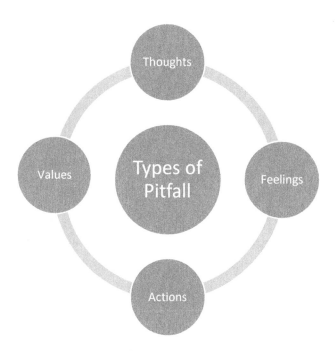

Thoughts

The main pitfall when it comes to thinking is not doing any! Reflective practice teaches us about the importance of carefully thinking through the issues we are involved with, drawing on our professional knowledge base, rather than relying on habit, guesswork or simply copying others. However, a common pitfall is for pressure of work to lead us into a non-reflective approach, potentially rushing about trying to get so much stuff done without a clear focus or a clear basis of understanding.

Unfortunately, I have come across a number of situations where this is precisely what has happened, where: (i) pressures of work have created a vicious circle in which too much pressure leads to a non-reflective, rushing about approach: (ii) a non-reflective approach is likely to be ineffective, if not positively dangerous, leading to more pressure; and (iii) additional pressures can lead to stress and more rushing about (see Section 27).

Supervision can be an important antidote to this, but not everyone is fortunate enough to receive good-quality reflective supervision that encourages us to think, plan analyse and learn. This does not mean that we cannot avoid a non-thinking response without good-quality supervision; it just makes it somewhat harder, and therefore all the more important that we do not lose sight of the need for reflective practice in general and critically reflective practice in particular.

Teamwork can also be important in this regard. Where there is little or no team support, non-reflective approaches can become more likely, as people go their separate ways and do little or nothing to help one another make sense of the complexities they are dealing with. By contrast, where there is good teamwork, a stimulating atmosphere can develop in which members are encouraged to think and make sense of the situations they are wrestling with, rather than just dive into them unthinkingly and hope for the best. Doing your best to support and sustain teamwork is therefore very important.

❖❖❖ KEY POINT ❖❖❖

Teamwork is an extension of the idea of partnership – it revolves around being able to work together effectively to achieve common goals and to manage any conflicts that may be standing in the way of arriving at the outcomes we are working towards.

Being a thoughtful, well-informed practitioner is what reflective practice is all about. The moment we abandon reflective practice and try to bypass the thinking aspects of our work, we place ourselves in a very dangerous place.

Feelings

Emotion-related pitfalls can apply to both the feelings of others and our own. It is worth exploring each of these in turn. First, when it comes to other people's feelings, there is a danger that we can:

- *Ignore those feelings* – perhaps because we are busy, in a rush, tired, distracted or otherwise not on top form. Similarly, we may miss the significance of feelings associated with grief, given the common tendency for loss and grief issues to be marginalized (see Section 21).

- *Misread those feelings* – especially in complex, highly sensitive situations with mixed emotions and/or emotions running high (situations involving abuse, for example). We have to be careful not to jump to conclusions about people's feelings.

- *Impose our own feelings* – for example, if we allow our own feelings of negativity to drag other people down (as so often happens in organizational cultures characterized by low morale).

 'Emotional intelligence' became a fashionable buzzword idea at one point, but we should not allow this to distract attention from the importance of being very skilled in dealing with emotional challenges, our own and other people's.

When it comes to our own feelings, we need to make sure that we do not:

- *Lose control* – we cannot help others to manage their feelings positively and constructively if we are allowing our own feelings to run wild. This is not about being expected to be unfeeling, but about having the 'emotional intelligence' to be able to keep our emotions in check as appropriate.

- *Lose sight of our feelings* – what we do in any situation will depend on not only what we think, but also what we feel. If we are not aware of what those feelings are and how they are affecting us, we are in a weak position to make a positive difference. This is an important aspect of self-awareness.

- *Allow anxiety to dominate* – anxiety protects us from danger by acting as a sort of 'early warning system'. However, if we are not careful, it can become a major problem, a vicious circle in which one person makes another anxious; the second person can make others anxious; and then anxiety can become a common feature of a situation or even an organizational culture. In some places a high level of anxiety can become the norm and thereby distort our priorities, our assessment of risk and therefore the quality of our work.

Actions

'You can't please all the people all the time' is a well-known adage, and it is certainly true in social work. So, one of the pitfalls to avoid is overstretching ourselves by trying to do too much for too many people. It is inevitable in social work that demand will outstrip supply much of the time and we will have to draw a line in terms of what we can do to help and what we can't. Elsewhere, I have referred to this as 'humility' – being humble about our limitations (Thompson, 2016d).

One thing that can stand in the way of avoiding this pitfall is a sedimentation model of social work (Thompson, 2016c), by which I mean the dangerous assumption that the role of social workers is to fill all the gaps left by the other public services – to deal with whatever is left after other professionals have drawn lines around what they can or cannot do. This type of model is highly dangerous because:

- It creates false expectations and, in effect, sets us up to fail, as we could not possibly fill all those gaps.

- It can create dependency by giving people the impression that, whatever the problem may be, a social worker will be able to help them with it.

- It stands in the way of systematic, outcome-focused practice by preventing us from being focused and specific in our work – our roles become too generalized.

- It devalues what we have to offer as human services professionals – it relegates us to the status of sweeping up after the 'real' professionals have done their jobs. It fails to take account of the *specific* benefits we can bring to people's problems and challenges.

What we need to do therefore is to make sure that we are being realistic in terms of what we can achieve, recognize the boundaries of our role and not allow others (members of the public, other professionals or the media) to push us into an unhelpful sedimentation way of working. Once again, it takes us back to the importance of 'setting out our stall' as part of our commitment to working in partnership.

Another important pitfall to avoid in terms of our actions is that of practising defensively. In Section 8 I emphasized the importance of professional accountability – this is a question of making our practice defensible, not defensive. Similarly, I highlighted the dangers in Section 22 of a risk-averse approach that encourages defensiveness. What is needed is proper professional accountability rooted in our knowledge, skills and values, and not a defensive 'cover your back' approach that involves losing sight of that knowledge, those skills and those values.

Values

As we have noted, values motivate and sustain us. They also help to ensure that we act responsibly, especially when we are exercising power. One potential major pitfall, therefore, is that we lose sight of our values, we allow pressure of work or other distractions to take us down a path that is driven by considerations other than our values.

This can happen in a number of ways, including the following:

➤ *Not tackling discrimination* Discrimination operates in subtle and complex ways. Very many people who are not tuned in to the significance of discrimination can fail to recognize when discrimination is occurring and will therefore not appreciate the harm done by the oppression it causes. Of course, as social workers, given our commitment to equality, diversity and social justice, we should be more tuned in to these issues than most. However, there may be times when we let such matters slip. For example, I have seen care proceedings reports relating to children that paid little or no attention to issues of race, culture, ethnicity and identity; files relating to older people that have clearly not taken ageism into account in the assessment(s) therein; and case records relating to women experiencing depression that have failed to incorporate important gender dimensions of the situation.

Part of the reason for this is that, in my experience, many people are able to conceptualize discrimination at a theoretical level and can thereby show a good understanding in principle. But, when it comes to day-to-day practice relating to situations in which discrimination is so common, they fail to spot it. This reflects the fact that, despite the oppressive consequences of discrimination, it is part of everyday life at personal, cultural and structural levels. It is therefore essential that we do not become blasé or let our guard down. We need to be alert at all times to discriminatory processes that are operating 'in plain sight'.

➢ *Becoming a 'culture victim'* I have already made the point that organizational cultures are powerful influences on workplace behaviour and interactions. This can help or hinder, depending on the nature of the culture is (what its unwritten rules and taken-for-granted assumptions are). At times, cultures can lead to behaviours that are not consistent with our values. For example, confidentiality may not be respected in a culture that is very lax about such matters. Likewise, a negative culture may lead to low morale and cynicism, thereby undermining a commitment to professionalism.

In particular, we need to guard against consumerist cultures – that is, those that see social work largely as a matter of rationing scarce resources and providing or commissioning services (as far as the budget will allow). A consumerist culture is one that has lost sight of problem solving and empowerment, offers no creativity or innovation, stifles learning and lowers morale. It is therefore essential that we guard against any such cultures if they begin to arise and do our best to go beyond them and eliminate them where they already exist.

*** KEY POINT ***

Consumerist cultures have arisen in public services as a byproduct of neoliberalism as a political and economic philosophy. Neoliberalism places great emphasis on relying on the market as a determining factor, the results of which include greater inequality and a lower level of investment in public services.

250

I have run very many training courses where we have had a long discussion about the influence of culture and, every time this has happened, the conclusion has been that cultures are indeed very powerful and it is certainly the case that they can act as a barrier to practising in ways that are consistent with social work values.

As I have consistently argued over the years, and will no doubt continue to do so, cultures are very powerful influences, but they are not all-powerful, we can bypass those influences if we so choose, however difficult that may be at times.

 Ask yourself which is the stronger influence on your practice, your professional values or the culture you work in? If it is the latter, you are in a very dangerous situation. Think carefully about the consequences of this.

It is understandable that people will be influenced by the culture they work in. However, if that culture is a barrier to practice based on integrity, we need to make sure that we do not become passive victims of that culture.

Conclusion

What we have explored are just some of the possible pitfalls we are likely to encounter. There are plenty of others. But, the key point I want you to take away from this is that we have to be on our guard constantly against such problems. We need to be alert and mindful; we need to make reflective practice a central part of our approach to our work: intelligent, well-informed practice rooted in our professional knowledge, skills and values. It won't guarantee a pitfall-free career, but it will stand us in very good stead in terms of the challenges we face.

Pitfalls to Avoid Exercise

What do you see as the *three* pitfalls you are most likely to face as challenges for you personally? What can you do to equip yourself as fully as possible to avoid them and/or deal with them if they do arise?

27. Surviving and thriving

Anyone who comes into social work expecting it to be an easy ride or a cushy number is in for a big surprise. Social work is very challenging work, but that is a big part of what makes it such rewarding and important work. We do important work in difficult circumstances, and so there is always a danger that those circumstances will overwhelm us and we will experience stress or burnout. So, in this section, we explore what is involved in making sure that we not only survive, but also thrive.

First of all, we will look at issues to do with motivation and morale (things that help us move forward) and then move on to consider stress and burnout (things that hold us back). A key message to take away from this section is the importance of self-care.

Motivation and morale

The terms, 'motivation' and 'morale' are often used interchangeably and, while they are certainly related, they are not the same thing. This is because motivation is a psychological matter – it relates to individuals – while morale is a sociological matter – it relates to groups of people, such as teams, and the culture in which those groups operate. Let's consider each of them in turn.

Motivation refers to what 'moves' us, what gives us the desire to engage in a particular activity. To feel motivated is to feel energized. We can understand motivation as comprising three different, but interacting elements:

- *Motivating factors* These are the things that will energize us. They may be tangible rewards, like money, or less tangible, but no less powerful rewards like job satisfaction and a sense of pride. Motivating factors are many and varied.

- *Demotivating factors* Also known as 'drag factors', these are the things that hold us back and reduce our motivation. They sap our energy and our resolve. It may be too much paperwork, long and tedious unproductive meetings or various other things. Demotivating factors are also many and varied.

- *Hygiene factors* This is not a matter of cleanliness, but there is a parallel. A hygiene factor is something that will not motivate us if present, but will demotivate us if absent. A simple example would be a desk. Being provided with a desk is not likely to motivate people, but in those offices where people are required to do 'hot desking', the absence of a desk can be a definite negative when it comes to motivation. The parallel with hygiene in the everyday sense is that cleanliness will not make us well, but its absence can make us ill.

One important point to emphasize about motivation is that it is our own personal responsibility. We are acting in bad faith if we sit back and expect others to do the motivating for us. Similarly, we will often be appealing to clients to take ownership of their motivation – for example, in making any changes that are necessary. Indeed, it could be argued that one person cannot motivate another; they can only create the circumstances in which the other person motivates him- or herself.

Morale is closely linked to motivation, but is a broader concept. Morale is a matter of shared culture. *I* have motivation, but *we* have morale. It refers to the mood or ethos within a team or group of people. It can be positive and energizing, as in good teamwork and leadership, and thereby contribute positively to motivation – it is empowering. It can also be negative and demoralizing, as in poor or non-existent teamwork and leadership, and thereby contribute negatively to motivation – it is disempowering.

While morale is a shared, sociological phenomenon, each of us as individuals will play a part in it, as cultures are the sum total of the actions and interactions of its members. Once again, we would be acting in bad faith if we were to assume that we have no role to play in shaping the culture and the level of morale within it.

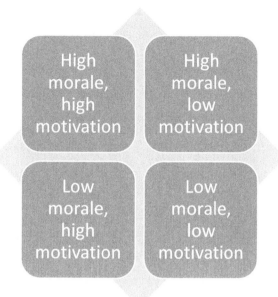

If we look carefully at the grid above, what we will see are the four possible combinations of motivation and morale:

- *High morale, high motivation* (top-left-hand corner). This is what we need to aim for – a culture that supports and facilitates motivation, with motivated people working in it.

- *High morale, low motivation* (top-right-hand corner). If someone's motivations remains low in a high-morale culture, this strongly suggests that there is something wrong, something that needs to be addressed. It prompts us to ask: What is preventing this person from being motivated and what can be done to help? It may be that they are experiencing personal problems at home, for example.

- *High motivation, low morale* (bottom left-hand corner). This refers to a situation where one or more people are managing to remain motivated, despite low morale. This can be difficult to achieve, but is certainly not impossible. The people who succeed in this regard deserve credit for it.

- *Low motivation, low morale* (bottom-right-hand corner). This is the worst-case scenario, where people have become 'culture victims'. Low motivation and low morale reinforce one another and the result is a highly problematic workplace, where there is the potential for everyone to lose out, especially the people we serve.

It should be clear, then, that anything other than high morale and high motivation presents us with challenges that we need to respond to – individually and collectively – as best we can.

A key point in this regard is the need to recognize that: (i) while moaning and expressing negative emotions ('ventilating', to give it its technical name), can have some value, if this becomes the norm, it creates and sustains a culture of negativity and low morale, thereby making a bad situation worse – it is disempowering; and (ii) if we, by contrast, commit ourselves to doing the best we can in difficult circumstances (which very accurately characterizes social work), then we contribute to creating and sustaining a culture of positivity and high morale – it is empowering.

>>> Moccasins moment <<<

Imagine you were receiving help from a professional whose heart is clearly not in their work and you were not happy about it. If they explained that they were demotivated because they work in a low-morale culture, would you think that was an acceptable reason?

Stress and burnout

In everyday speech, stress and pressure are used interchangeably, but, like motivation and morale, if we want to get a fuller, more professional understanding, we need to be clear about the important distinction between them.

Pressure is neutral, in the sense that it can be either positive (energizing, rewarding, enjoyable) or negative (harmful, distressing, demoralizing), depending on the level, intensity, type and duration of the pressure and the quality and quantity of support we receive. Stress, by contrast, in its technical sense, refers to situations in which pressure is harming us in some way (our health, our well-being, our relationships, our quality and quantity of work and so on).

The UK Health and Safety Executive define stress as what we experience when the level of pressure exceeds our ability to cope with it (http://www.hse.gov.uk/stress/what-to-do.htm). This is an important definition, partly because it helps us challenge the myth that 'stress is good for you' (a myth that is often used to play down the seriousness of stress  as a problem in the workplace), and partly because it helps us to realize that we should not confuse pressure with stress. Social work is, by its very nature, definitely a pressurized undertaking, but is not necessarily stressful. Indeed, for the most part, social workers are extremely skilled in coping with significant levels of pressure (and helping others to do so).

However, social work is not, by its very nature, stressful, but it can become stressful when workloads are too high and/or expectations are unrealistic; support is lacking or even counterproductive; where there is workplace bullying; where there is a lack of leadership, leaving people feeling unsupported, unappreciated and unsafe. It is essential that we recognize this point and do not make the mistake of assuming that 'social work is stressful' (which contributes to stress being seen as normal and inevitable when it is not). Social work is certainly pressurized, but those pressures can be positive and rewarding. Social work only becomes stressful when the circumstances in which it is being carried out are problematic in one or more ways. If we come to see social work as stressful *per se*, we will fail to appreciate the need to tackle the circumstances that lead to stress. We disempower ourselves in circumstances that are already disempowering.

Burnout is commonly understood as a form of stress, whereas in reality it is a way (albeit a very unhelpful way) of responding to stress. Someone who is burnt out is a person who has responded to stress by developing a sort of protective skin that, in a sense, numbs them to feelings and thereby protects them from the pain of stress. It is like a form of depression in some ways. What makes it doubly dangerous is: (i) anyone practising from a position of burnout is likely to be practising dangerously; and (ii) it 'seals us in' to stress, in the sense that it cuts us off from ways of tackling the problems that led to the stress in the first place. It is a form of defeatism.

What is vitally important in relation to both stress and burnout is self-care, and so we need to be clear about what is involved in that.

Self-care

One of the 'occupational hazards' of social work is that our desire and determination to help other people with their problems, needs and challenges can so easily lead us into neglecting our own problems, needs and challenges. We are going to be of very little use to anyone if we put ourselves at risk by neglecting our own self-care.

Self-care is a complex matter, but the following guidelines can be helpful:

- At all times be aware of your own self-care needs. You do nobody any favours by neglecting them.

- Do not be afraid to ask for support when you need it.
- Be realistic about what you can achieve; do not spread yourself too thinly.
- Don't set yourself up to fail by expecting to have a 100% success rate.
- Don't lose sight of your values; they are a significant source of motivation.
- Celebrate and value your successes, however small they may seem at the time.
- Manage your pressures as effectively as you can – do not let them manage you.

An important underpinning of self-care is keeping a firm grip on our professionalism, while also recognizing that we have a life of our own, that we have work-life balance to keep in check.

Surviving or thriving?

Over the years I have had very many conversations with practitioners where they have been asking my advice about how to *survive* in social work, how to keep on top of things. I have always answered in the same way by advising them to focus not on *surviving*, but on *thriving* – to look at how they can do the best job possible, not just one that is good enough. If we focus on 'just getting through the day' we are being unduly negative, with the result that small problems can loom large and big positives can be scaled down or left out of the picture altogether.

Part of being a professional is setting out to do the best we possibly can, rather than just settle for what is acceptable. That is basically what thriving is about, and if we can get the thriving right, we don't need to worry about the surviving bit as that comes with it as a matter of course.

Surviving and Thriving Exercise

What are the things that motivate you about social work? How can you make the most of these? What are the things that can demotivate you? What can you do to avoid these or minimize their impact? What hygiene factors can you identify? Is there anything you can do about these?

28. Managing your placement experience

This section, specifically for social work students, is designed to help you get the most out of the part of your education and training that you spend on placement. Social workers involved in delivering practice learning may also find it of interest.

It is divided into three parts. In the first one we look at the importance of clarifying expectations, including having a clear learning agreement or contract. This is followed by an overview of the importance of focusing on learning and not getting sidetracked by worrying too much about being assessed. We then examine the central role of supervision and help you understand what your role is in making this a success.

Clarifying expectations

Just being in a social work setting for a number of weeks will present you with a number of learning opportunities, but there is so much more that can be achieved in terms of your learning if you have a helpful learning agreement. This should be developed between you and the person supervising you (variously known in

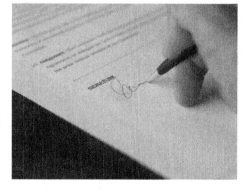

different contexts as a practice teacher, practice assessor, practice educator, field supervisor and other such terms). It should identify what you are hoping to learn. While this can include general terms, it should not be limited to these – the more specific you can be the better, so you will need to think carefully about this. But you needn't wrestle with this on your own – feel free to get help from anyone you feel may be able to support you in thinking these issues through.

It can also be helpful for your learning agreement to specify *how* it is expected that you will be able to achieve the learning you have identified. What steps will need to be taken? What opportunities will need to be organized or accessed? Again, the more specific you can be, the better.

Clarification can also be helpful in terms of:

- *Induction* Where will you sit? What about parking or transport links? What policies and procedures will you need to be aware of? Who will you need to meet? Why?

- *Practicalities* How often will supervision sessions take place? When and at what venue? What preparation will be required? (see the discussion of using supervision below).

- *Workload* What will your workload comprise of? How will it be chosen? Will it match your learning needs?

- *Support* Is there any additional support available – for example, for students with disabilities or from a minority ethnic group? Are there other students nearby who could perhaps form the basis of an informal student support group?

- *The role of the team* Will team members be involved in supporting your learning (more than just being good colleagues)? If so, how? Are there specific ways in which you can benefit from the experience and expertise of colleagues?

- *Things going wrong* If things are not working out for any reason, what should happen? What is the role of the tutor?

Not all of these would need to be included in a learning agreement, but it is none the less important for you and your supervisor to have clarity about the issues involved. This may not be possible from Day One of the placement, but it is important not to let time drift and delay getting things clarified. A lack of clarity causes confusion and tension, and confusion and tension get in the way of learning.

Focusing on learning

The majority of practice placements are assessed – that is, there is an expectation that the student will demonstrate evidence of competence and understanding in relation to a number of predefined areas. Such a framework of assessment can be a very helpful spur to learning, as it provides a structure to work to and clarity about what is expected. However, there is also the potential for it to become a barrier to learning. This is because being assessed can generate anxiety, and anxiety is also something that can get in the way of learning, especially if that anxiety sets off a vicious circle in which more and more anxiety is generated, potentially creating a panic response.

*** KEY POINT ***

Anxiety is basically a response to perceived threat. It is an early warning system alerting us to potential danger. As such, it is a useful and positive mechanism. However, a common problem encountered in social work is that, if we are not careful, 'anxiety begets anxiety' – that is, it spirals out of control. Awareness of anxiety and the ability to keep it within manageable proportions are therefore important parts of a social worker's repertoire.

So, the first point for me to emphasize is that you must not let the assessment create undue anxiety in you. I say 'undue', because a small and manageable amount of anxiety is not a problem and can actually be a source of motivation. What we have to bear in mind is that being able to manage anxiety (our own and other people's) is a very important social work skill, so this is a good time to start developing that skill if you are not already very capable in that department.

One very important consideration in this regard is the need for you to focus on the learning first and foremost and not make the assessment your priority. Put it this way, if you focus mainly on learning, you are *increasing* your chances significantly of being able to demonstrate competence as required, and thereby passing your placement. However, if you are focusing primarily on being assessed, you will be holding your learning back and, in so doing, *decreasing* your chances of being able to demonstrate competence as required, and thereby making it more likely that you will fail the placement.

So, the irony is that, if you focus mainly on assessment (at the expense of learning), you make it *more likely* that you will have problems with that assessment. By contrast, if you focus mainly on learning, you make it *less likely* that you will have problems with the assessment.

Placements are an excellent chance to develop your knowledge, skills and confidence and to develop a better understanding of values and their significance. There will, of course, be some very practical learning, such as being taught how to use the agency's computer system, finding out which forms need to be completed and in what circumstances, and so on. But your learning should extend far beyond that – you should also be broadening and deepening your knowledge of a wide range of social work issues. Just as importantly, you should also be able to bring to life the theory you have been learning about, to see how the ideas you have been reading about and discussing fit into the world of actual practice.

Unfortunately, some people try to keep theory and practice separate – theory, according to them, is what you talk about in essays and assignments, but is not something that has a place in the world of practice. Of course, this is a dangerous approach to adopt, as it leaves us ill-equipped to make sense of the complexities of practice. What is much wiser is to use a placement as a way of exploring how what is taught in the academic setting can give us useful insights into people's lives, their problems, the potential solutions, the strengths they can draw upon and what we can potentially do to help within a framework of skills, values and ethics and an understanding of the wider sociopolitical context. That is what I mean by bringing the theory to life.

In this way, placements give us a foundation from which to develop our critically reflective practice skills. This is in large part why it is important to embrace fully the new learning opportunities presented by the placement experience and taking the chance to integrate them with the learning you have already done in the academic setting – and indeed from your life experience to date.

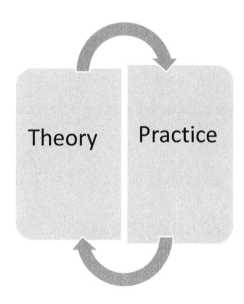

Using supervision

Supervision is an important process in both social work practice and social work education. It is intended to help in four ways:

➢ *Accountability* Supervision should help to ensure that you are working within the appropriate legal, policy and ethical boundaries. This is for everyone's protection, yours, the organization's and, most of all, the people we serve. This is likely to involve you receiving advice and guidance appropriate to the situations you are dealing with. This can be a very positive and constructive way of learning, although some people can feel uncomfortable in what they may perceive as a process of being checked up on, and may therefore become defensive. There is no need for this, as it is part of your supervisor's job, and this type of supervisory accountability applies to qualified social workers too.

> *Learning and development* Supervision is about helping you to be the best worker you can be. So, it will include helping you to maximize your learning. This will involve allocating you a suitable amount of work at a level of difficulty appropriate to your experience and level of development. It will also involve drawing out the lessons to be learned from the work you do, helping you to draw links between the work you are doing and your academic learning (integrating theory and practice again). It may also involve setting project work for you, recommending reading and/or putting you in touch with individuals or organizations that can help you with your learning and development.

> *Well-being* Your supervisor will not be your counsellor, nurse or parent, but they will want to make sure that your well-being is being safeguarded. It goes back to the question of helping you to be the best worker you can be. If you are stressed, unduly anxious or otherwise having difficulties, you will not be achieving your best. A good supervisor should help you feel supported, valued and safe. To enable them to do this, you will need to be open with them and steer clear of defensiveness – it is important that the supervisory relationship is based on mutual trust.

> *Mediation* Conflicts can also stand in the way of you achieving your best, so supervision can be a very useful place to identify and address any such conflicts (see Section 20).

An important point about supervision to emphasize is that it is a two-way professional process, not a one-way bureaucratic one. It is two way in the sense that you have to play your part; you have to participate fully (for example, by preparing for each session so that you make the best use of the supervision time available) – it is something you and your supervisor engage in together, rather than something that is done to you. It is a professional process because it is geared towards helping you be the best (professional) worker you can be, and not just a process of being checked up on. If you bear this key point in mind it will stand you in good stead.

Supervision			
Accountability	Learning and development	Well-being	Mediation

Conclusion

When handled properly by all involved, placements can offer incredibly rich learning experiences. This section will not guarantee a successful and worthwhile placement, but it should give you a helpful foundation on which to build.

29. Managing your career

Many people think of their job as just a way of putting food on the table and paying their bills, with no sense of career or career development. The professional nature of social work presents us with a different picture, though, with a clear expectation that what we are doing is more than a job, it is a vocation – and implicit within that is the idea of continuous development. As we noted in Section 8, this is not just a matter of attending a training course from time to time; it is a commitment to continuing to learn and develop throughout our working life, to strive to do our very best, to achieve the optimal standards that we are capable of.

Assuming that it is acceptable to be static and settle for doing a job that is just about good enough is not compatible with the professionalism on which social work is based. It reflects losing sight of our values and the important role of social work in contributing to making our society a humane one. So, in this section, our emphasis is on clarifying what is involved in the notion of having a career and what is involved in managing your career.

What is a career?

Literally a career is a pathway. The word comes from the same Latin roots as 'cart'. So, what it refers to basically is a way forward, the path we choose to follow through our working lives.

We can, of course, change career pathway during our working years, and many people do. Indeed, there are very many people in the social work field who have had other careers first, often careers that they did not find challenging enough, hence the attraction of the demanding nature of social work for many.

Traditionally, the concept of career has been thought of as a ladder, with career progression seen as primarily, if not exclusively, in terms of promotion – the next step on the ladder. This can be problematic in (at least) four ways:

- It neglects the importance of thinking about a career in horizontal terms, not just vertical (I will return to this point below).

- As organizations increasingly have 'flatter' structures (that is, fewer layers of management) than used to be the case, opportunities for promotion become fewer, hence more competitive, and can thereby create a lot of tension and additional pressure in what is already a pressurized occupation.

- Focusing on promotion can distort our priorities and stand in the way of our professionalism. For example, some people can become ruthless in their pursuit of promotion and thereby destroy teamwork and lose sight of what social work is all about.

- I have come across many people who have been promoted and subsequently regretted it, finding that they were much happier in their previous job. Some have had the courage and integrity to return to their previous level when the situation has arisen, but many have remained unhappy in their higher role, feeling trapped there.

>>> Moccasins moment <<<

If you or your family were receiving help from a social worker or other professional and it was apparent that they have one eye on promotion and are not fully focused on being helpful, how would you feel about this? What effect would it have on your respect for that person?

However, it does not have to be this way. There is nothing inherent in the notion of career progression that requires promotion to be part of it. We can also think of career progression in developmental terms, including both personal and professional development. By including personal development, what I am saying is that a career can offer the opportunity for each of us to grow as a person, rather than simply get better at our jobs. In a person-centred profession like social work, this is particularly appropriate.

Upwards or onwards?

Career progression can be vertical (promotion up the ladder) or horizontal (capitalizing on development opportunities) or a mixture of the two. Horizontal or developmental career progression includes a wide range of possibilities, such as the following:

➤ *Maximizing learning* Simply continuing to learn and thereby becoming increasingly competent and effective in your work is in itself a positive form of career progression. This could be pursued formally – for example, through studying for a higher qualification – or informally through self-directed learning (see the discussion of this in Section 30). There is also much to be learned from reflective practice, especially if it is complemented by reflective supervision, and from in-service training opportunities. The difference in effectiveness between someone who seeks to maximize their learning and someone who settles for just getting the job done is immense, the gulf between them is huge.

➤ *Helping others learn* This can be done informally by just being a supportive colleague who mentors others – particularly less experienced colleagues -- helping them to learn and develop their confidence. It can also be done more formally by getting involved in practice learning when you have enough experience to do so. At some point, you may also be able to get involved in being a guest speaker at a university or contributing to your organization's in-service training programme. These can all be helpful, enjoyable and rewarding ways of contributing positively to your workplace and your own career development. This path is not for everyone, but many people have trodden it and been very glad they did.

➤ *Project work* From time to time there will be opportunities to get involved in a project of some kind – a working party, a service planning group or similar. These too can be enjoyable, useful and rewarding. These opportunities may arise within your own organization or within a multidisciplinary framework. If this kind of thing appeals to you, you may want to let it be known to the appropriate people that you would be interested in getting involved if a suitable opportunity arises.

➤ *Union or professional association work* Professional associations and unions present a wide range of opportunities to get involved in activities that help to  promote and develop social work and to serve to protect social workers. These can help to enrich your working life, broaden your outlook, provide stimulation and give you the opportunity to get the rewards and satisfactions of making a positive contribution to your fellow professionals and indeed to our profession itself.

➤ *Research and publication* From time to time there may be opportunities to get engaged in research projects, and there is always the possibility of working with colleagues to initiate some sort of research. That may sound daunting, but when you are experienced and confident enough, and when you have suitable colleagues to work with, research can be very rewarding and worthwhile – and it does not have to be a major project. There will also be opportunities to write for publication – for example, your professional organization's member magazine and/or relevant professional websites. You don't have to be the world's best writer, you just need to have something important to say – and, as a values-driven professional, you should have plenty to say. Whether your involvement is to be in research, in publications or both, you will need to discuss your plans with your employer so that they are aware of what is happening.

If we think of our career as a journey, a pathway through our working life, then we can think of career progression in terms of a process of enriching that journey as fully as possible, gaining the greatest satisfaction, maximizing our learning and development and making the best positive contribution we can to making our society a more humane one.

 Beware of the pressure to think of career success narrowly in terms of promotion. Promotion can be a wonderful thing, but making it the be all and end all of your career plan is highly problematic.

So, it is essential to recognize that moving forward in your career is not necessarily about moving upwards. It is about having a fulfilling and rewarding career, whether or not that involves increasing your salary or your level of power and responsibility.

The importance of consolidation

We have noted some of the dangers associated with the tendency to equate career progression with promotion. A further danger is that it can lead to a failure to consolidate learning and quality of practice. I have come across a number of people whose ambitions have led them to seek promotion at the earliest opportunity, reaching the next level on the ladder without first developing a strong, consolidated foundation of understanding and experience on their existing rung. For example, a participant on a training course once told me that, when she was at university, her tutor had served as a qualified social worker for only 18 months before being appointed as a tutor. The participant went on to say that the tutor's lack of experience was reflected in the quality of her teaching and her tutorial support.

 Learning is not necessarily fixed and forever. We can learn something, by being involved in a complex, multi-level case, for example, but if we don't reinforce and build on that learning, it may well fade away, and we thereby lose the benefit of that experience and that learning. If learning is not *consolidated*, it will be of only short-term value. However, if we reinforce and extend that learning through further experience, further use of that knowledge and further reflective practice, we ensure a much more robust and lasting foundation of knowledge. Someone constantly in a hurry to get to the next level is likely to risk missing out on that consolidation and leave themselves in a much weaker position to fulfil their duties.

A lack of consolidation is not only a problem for the individuals concerned, but also for those who work with them. For example, someone who is promoted to a management position without first having established a firm, consolidated basis of knowledge and understanding (and the confidence that goes with it) may leave their supervisees inadequately supported. This can lead to a vicious circle. If supervisees lose respect for, and confidence in, their manager, the subsequent loss of credibility for that manager can leave them ill-equipped to do their job effectively, leading to a loss of confidence on their part (and/or manipulative game playing to try and conceal their lack of confidence and knowledge), which in turn will reduce their credibility and thus their ability to influence people in a positive direction (see the discussion of subjective and objective confidence in Section 3).

Consolidation is therefore an important part of career development if we are to avoid the problems outlined here.

Conclusion

I want to emphasize that I am not trying to discourage anyone from applying for promotion when the time is right, but what I am doing is stressing that we need to move away from the common narrow definition of career progression as promotion after promotion. As we have seen, this is problematic, not least because such a 'vertical' approach can lead to people missing out on the range of 'horizontal' opportunities for career enhancement, job satisfaction and a fulfilling working life.

Managing Your Career Exercise

Imagine that you are at or near the end of your career looking back over what you have achieved in your working life. What would the important things be? What would matter most to you? Once you are clear about this you can make sure that you don't lose sight of these important issues as you progress through your career.

30. Keeping the learning going

Unfortunately, a lot of people in social work and, indeed, in other professional groups have a tendency to 'plateau' – that is, to learn, develop and improve until they reach a certain level of competence and then develop no further. As we have noted, this is not consistent with professionalism, and nor is it the most productive approach to working life. As I mentioned in Section 8, it is sometimes referred to as 'satisficing' – settling for 'good enough', rather than aiming for 'best possible'.

So, in this section, we are going to explore why it is important to keep the learning going, what can get in the way of such learning and what can be done to maximize our learning. I also take the opportunity to emphasize the importance of self-directed learning.

The importance of learning

We have already acknowledged that continuous learning is a professional expectation: continuous improvement is what is called for. The longer we are in a job, the better we should be at it.

But this is not the only reason. We should also be aware of the following:

- *Use it or lose it* As we noted in the discussion of consolidation in Section 29, if we do not build on our learning and keep it going, much of it will fade away.

- *Managing complexity* Professional practice can be seen as an intellectual activity, one that requires well-developed analytical skills to do justice to the complex issues involved. We therefore need to keep our thinking cogs well oiled and in constant use.

- *Confidence* Personal and professional growth can fuel confidence, but where there is no such growth, confidence can either wither or become complacency, as we get more and more rusty.

No one is perfect, and so there is always room for improvement, and social work, as such a challenging activity, offers no shortage of opportunities for learning and development.

Obstacles to learning

Balanced against the value and importance of keeping the learning going must be the acknowledgement that there exist a number of obstacles to learning, including the following:

- *Becoming a culture victim* We have already discussed the dangers of abandoning our professionalism and just following the crowd by allowing a workplace culture to be dictating how we practise. A culture that does not support learning can therefore hold us back significantly.

- *Neglecting reflective practice* Due to time pressures people will often say that they do not have time for reflection, without realizing that when we are under a lot of pressure is precisely the time when we need to be *more* reflective, not *less* so.

- *Losing sight of the bigger picture* It is very easy for busy people to focus narrowly on the details of whatever situation they are dealing with and lose sight of the bigger picture. In doing so, they are losing sight of their wider learning.

- *No longer reading* We are very fortunate in social work to have a huge literature available to us across a range of social science disciplines, but it never ceases to amaze me how many social workers seem to think that, once they qualify, they have no need of further reading.

- *Anxiety and low confidence* Anxiety is likely to distract us and thereby block learning, while a lack of confidence is highly likely to have a similar effect.

This is not an exhaustive list, but it is certainly enough to alert us to the fact that there are many ways in which our learning can be stymied, and so we need to tune in to this situation and actively guard against falling foul of any of these.

Making learning happen

What follows in terms of steps we can take to make sure we keep the learning going throughout our career is not an exhaustive list either, but again some issues that we need to be aware of.

➢ *Professional assertiveness* In contemporary social work we face many pressures to adopt a largely bureaucratic consumerist approach to practice that is not consistent with our values or, indeed, our professionalism. Professional assertiveness is the courage, the commitment and the set of skills we need to make sure that we remain true to the spirit of social work as a humanitarian endeavour geared towards problem solving, empowerment and social justice and not simply a process of rationing scarce resources and ticking boxes. Professional assertiveness also includes not allowing such

279

pressures to stand in the way of our learning. What we do in social work is important; continuing to learn is important; and so professional assertiveness is very important too.

➤ *Critically reflective practice* The importance of this should be crystal clear by now. The alternative is to practise with our brain in neutral, which is clearly a hazardous approach to the complex challenges of social work. If we are  thinking, planning and analysing and drawing on our professional knowledge base as we go about our business, then we will be generating a constant stream of opportunities for learning. Indeed, reflective practice and reflective learning go hand in hand.

➤ *Maintaining mental fitness* This is not about mental health. It is parallel with physical fitness. In physical terms, the more we exercise, the easier it gets and the more benefit we get from it. The same can be seen to apply to our mind. The more we exercise it through learning, the easier it becomes, the better we become at doing it and the more benefit we get from it. We therefore have to work hard to make sure that we do not allow ourselves (whatever the pressures to do so) to slip into unthinking routines on autopilot or just following the tramlines laid down by the culture we work in.

➤ *Keeping in touch with our values* Our values motivate us, sustain us, protect us (and others), but they can also help us learn. They give us a framework to guide our actions and can therefore be understood as a helpful basis for learning. For example, our values can guide us through complex and sensitive matters relating to discrimination and oppression. They do not give us answers on a plate, but they provide us with useful 'thinking tools' that can help us wrestle with the subtleties involved.

➤ *Connecting with like-minded people* You may be lucky enough to work in a culture where there is a strong commitment to learning and development, and then you can benefit by having the support of others as part of a shared endeavour of maximizing learning and thereby achieving the best standards of practice possible. However, if you are not lucky enough to work in such a culture, you should still be able to get the support of like-minded people who are also committed to learning, but you will need to seek them out. Making the effort to do so will certainly stand you in good stead in developing a network of people who can support you (and you can support them) in taking learning forward.

*** KEY POINT ***

Learning is often presented as if it were a solo project, something we need to do largely on our own. However, in reality, much learning is *social* in nature, developed through interactions with others. We should not underestimate the learning that can be gained from other people and their perspectives.

Self-directed learning

Most formal learning input is planned, designed and delivered by someone other than the learner. Someone else is in the driving seat. While this can work well on many occasions, it is far from ideal. It is not surprising, then, that there is now a growing emphasis on, and interest in, self-directed learning – learning in which you are in the driving seat in deciding what you want to learn and how you will learn it.

Of course, that is something that is quite difficult to do, but: (i) you don't have to do it alone – tutors, trainers, managers and other education and training professionals can act as mentors in supporting you in developing self-directed learning (instead of directing your learning for you) and, of course, there can also be 'peer mentoring' – that is, where individuals support each other in their learning; and (ii) as with most things, the more experience you gain of self-directed learning, the easier it gets.

Self-directed learning tends to be more effective than conventional approaches to learning because it is more *meaningful* to us, more closely suited to our own needs, circumstances, interests and preferences. It is about what matters to *you*. Deciding on your own learning pathway improves (i) motivation; and (ii) effectiveness

This also gets round the 'transfer of learning' problem associated with conventional training – that is, for much of the learning to be left behind in the training room and not actually implemented in practice,

My own contribution to promoting self-directed learning was to set up the Avenue Professional Development Programme, a subscription-based online learning community geared towards developing critically reflective practice via self-directed learning.

Discussion forums with tutor input ▲ an e-portfolio to record and consolidate learning ▲ a growing library of multimedia learning resources ▲ the *Learning to Learn* e-learning course ▲ two e-books, one to establish your learning pathway and another to review progress ▲ a reflective journal ▲ newsfeeds ▲ a virtual coffee shop with opportunities for online socializing

Primarily, self-directed learning involves taking ownership of your own learning and using whatever sources of support you can to help you take that learning forward. It is an *active* approach to learning, led by ourselves, rather than a *passive* one, led by others.

Conclusion

Learning can happen spontaneously at times, with little effort on our part. However, it is a big mistake to assume that this type of learning is enough. What is a much wiser approach is to recognize that the more active our approach to learning is, the more effective we will be, not only in that learning, but also in the quality of practice the learning is intended to enhance.

Keeping the learning going is a win-win situation all round. We benefit from our own learning; our colleagues can benefit too, especially if we work together as part of a learning culture; our managers benefit too, as they get better quality of work from us and help the team to be more fully effective; and our employing organization gets a better 'return on investment' in terms of their employment costs. But, most of all the people we serve benefit from the more professional service we are able to offer.

Keeping the Learning Going Exercise

What do you need to do to develop your self-directed learning capability? How can you move away from the mindset that someone else is in charge of your learning? Who can help you with this?

Conclusion

Social work is, by its very nature, challenging, in so far as it is concerned primarily with addressing people's problems, unmet needs, difficulties and distress. At times, the organizations that employ social workers – especially in a neoliberal context – can add to the challenges too, as can the distortions of those media that are more interested in making a profit than publishing the truth. So, we need to be clear that social work is not for the fainthearted; it is for people who relish a challenge, people who are prepared to commit fully to making a positive difference to the lives of some of the most disadvantaged members of our community and play a part in making our society a more humane one.

There are no easy answers to social work's challenges, no simple formulas to apply. It is about making sure that we are well equipped with a strong and growing knowledge base, a set of skills that we are constantly building and a set of values that motivate and sustain us and keep us safe and honest. All this needs to be underpinned by critically reflective practice – that is, by an intelligent, well-informed approach that enables us to make sense of complex situations and develop, in partnership, workable plans for addressing the issues we face.

We are fortunate enough to have a large literature base to draw upon and a strong basis of scholarship in the social sciences that can be of use. This manual has not been intended to add to that knowledge base, but, rather, to provide a helpful guide as to how to draw on aspects of that knowledge base in actual practice. In this respect, the manual offers a 'thinking tool'; it won't tell you what to do in certain circumstances, but it should give you a foundation of understanding to inform your steps towards critically reflective practice.

As I mentioned at the beginning, the manual is not comprehensive or exhaustive, as there is so much more that could be said. However, I very much hope that you will have found it beneficial and that you will continue to draw upon it throughout your career, rather than allow it to gather dust on a shelf.

As I have found myself saying so many times before: social work is important, which means that you are important, and so it is essential that you are as well equipped as possible for the challenges ahead. Please make sure that you make full use of whatever insights you have gained from this manual. Learning does not happen by magic, so please do make sure that you draw on the learning as much as possible. It matters.

Guide to further learning

The fact that I list items here means that I think the authors have something interesting or important to say. It does not mean that I necessarily agree with what they are saying or endorse their views or work. Similarly, it should not be assumed that anything I have omitted from this guide has little or no value or benefit. There is a wealth of useful material out there, and this guide necessarily has to be selective.

> Have I missed anything important? Are you aware of a text or a learning resource that you have found useful? Let me know about it and I will consider including it in a future edition.

Begin at the beginning

Some useful introductions to social work include my own *Understanding Social Work* (4th edn, Palgrave, 2015) plus:

Adams, R. (2010) *The Short Guide to Social Work*, Bristol, The Policy Press.

Doel, M. (2012) *Social Work: The Basics*, London, Routledge.

Parker, J. (2017) *Social Work Practice*, 5th edn, London, Sage.

There is also my e-book, *How to Do Social Work* (Avenue Media Solutions, 2015). In addition, a book that nicely gives the 'flavour' of social work is:

Doel, M. (ed.) (2017) *Social Work in 42 Objects (and more),* Lichfield, Kirwin Maclean Associates.

Attitudes and values

In my view, the best book on values is:

Moss, B. R. (2007) *Values*, Lyme Regis, Russell House Publishing.

Other useful texts include:

Banks. S. (2012) *Ethics and Values in Social Work*, 4th edn, Basingstoke, Palgrave Macmillan.

Doel, M. (2016) *Rights and Wrongs in Social Work*, London, Palgrave.

Hugman, R. and Carter, J. (eds) (2017) *Rethinking Values and Ethics in Social Work*, London, Palgrave.

Being prepared

The Knowledge | Skills | Values framework is discussed in *Understanding Social Work* and the Three Rs are discussed in *The Professional Social Worker* (2nd edn, Palgrave, 2016).

Making a difference

Theorizing practice is discussed in Chapter 1 of *Social Work Theories and Methods: The Essentials* (Thompson and Stepney, 2017) and more fully in my *Theorizing Practice* book (2nd edn, Palgrave, 2017).

Social work processes are discussed in my *People Skills* book (4th edn, Palgrave, 2015). Other useful books are:

Egan, G. (2017) *The Skilled Helper*, 2nd edn, Andover, Cengage.

Trevithick, P. (2012) *Social Work Skills and Knowledge,* 3rd edn, Maidenhead, Open University Press.

For social work tools, my *The People Solutions Sourcebook* (2nd edn, Palgrave Macmillan, 2012) is a useful starting point. Also of value are:

Mónnink, H. de (2017) *The Social Workers' Toolbox: Sustainable Multimethod Social Work,* London, Routledge.

Thompson, N. and Stepney, P. (eds) (2017) *Social Work Theories and Methods: The Essentials*, New York: Routledge.

Thinking holistically

The importance of a sociological approach is emphasized in my *Applied Sociology* book (Routledge, 2018).

In relation to the organizational context, an excellent textbook is:

Linstead, S., Fulop, L. and Lilley, S. (2009) *Management and Organization: A Critical Text*, 2nd edn, Basingstoke, Palgrave Macmillan.

There is also my own e-book on *Effective Teamwork* (Avenue Media Solutions, 2012).

The political context is well covered in:

Jordan, B. and Drakeford, M. (2013) *Social Work and Social Policy under Austerity,* Basingstoke, Palgrave Macmillan.

For the historical context of social work I would recommend:

Payne, M. (2005) *The Origins of Social Work: Continuity and Change,* Basingstoke, Palgrave Macmillan.

Working in partnership

The following text contains some very useful material on working together:

Glasby, J. and Dickinson, H. (2014) *Partnership Working in Health and Social Care: What Is Integrated Care and How Can We Deliver It?*, 2nd edn, Bristol, The Policy Press.

My *Effective Teamwork* e-book is also very relevant (see below).

Equality, diversity and social justice

This is one of my major interests, as is reflected in the number of publications I have in this field, primarily the following:

Thompson, N. (2007) *Power and Empowerment*, Lyme Regis, Russell House Publishing.

Thompson, N. (2016) *Anti-Discriminatory Practice: Equality, Diversity and Social Justice*, 6th edn, London, Palgrave.

Thompson, N. (2017) *Social Problems and Social Justice*, London, Palgrave.

Thompson, N. (2018) *Promoting Equality: Working with Diversity and Difference*, 4th edn, London, Palgrave.

Other useful sources include:

Dorling, D. (2015) *Injustice: Why Social Inequality Still Persists*, 2nd edn, Bristol, The Policy Press.

Mullaly, B. and West, J. (2017) *Challenging Oppression and Confronting Privilege: A Critical Approach to Anti-Oppressive and Anti-Privilege Theory and Practice*, 3rd edn, Don Mills, Canada, Oxford University Press.

Parker, J. and Ashencaen Crabtree, S. (2018) *Social Work with Marginalised and Disadvantaged People*, Sage, London.

Being a professional

My *The Professional Social Worker* (2nd edn, Palgrave, 2016) addresses these issues directly, emphasizing the importance of *authentic* professionalism. The following texts also have important things to say:

Cribb, A. and Gewirtz, S. (2015) *Professionalism*, Cambridge, Polity.

Parker, J. and Doel, M. (eds) (2013) *Professional Social Work*, London, Sage.

Duyvendak, J. W. Knijn, T. and Kremer, M. (eds) (2006) *Policy, People and the New Professional: De-professionalization and Re-professionalization in Care and Welfare*, Amsterdam, Amsterdam University Press.

Spirituality

I discuss the significance of spirituality in *The Professional Social Worker*. I would also want to highlight:

Gilbert, P. (ed.) (2011) *Spirituality and Mental Health*, Brighton, Pavilion.

Holloway, M. and Moss, B. (2010) *Spirituality and Social Work*, Basingstoke, Palgrave Macmillan.

Reflective practice

Unsurprisingly I would recommend *The Critically Reflective Practitioner* (Thompson and Thompson, 2018). My *Theorizing Practice* book is also very relevant. Schőn's original, highly influential text is also still worth investigating:

Schőn, D. A. (1983) *The Reflective Practitioner*, New York, Basic Books

Another interesting book is:

Ghaye, T. (2011) *Teaching and Learning through Reflective Practice*, London, Routledge.

Growth and change

There is a wealth of literature on child development and human development more broadly. Most of it adopts a narrow, bio-psychological approach, but one notable exception is:

Hunt, S. J. (2017) *The Life Course: A Sociological Introduction*, 2nd edn, London, Palgrave.

Some useful sources around facing death include:

Gawande, A. (2014) *Being Mortal*, London, Profile Books.

Kalanithi, P. (2016) *When Breath Becomes Air,* London, Bodley Head.

Yalom, I. D. (2011) *Staring at the Sun: Overcoming the Dread of Death*, London, Piatkus.

Health and well-being

Social aspects of health are well covered in:

Davidson, A. (2014) *Social Determinants of Health: A Comparative Approach*, Oxford, Oxford University Press.

A very important text on social work in relation to disability is:

Oliver, M., Sapey, B and Thomas, P. (2012) *Social Work with Disabled People*, 4th edn, Basingstoke, Palgrave Macmillan.

Social work and well-being are discussed in:

Jordan, B. (2007) *Social Work and Well-being*, Lyme Regis, Russell House Publishing.

An important text in relation to social work in mental health is:

Tew, J. (2011) *Social Approaches to Mental Distress*, Basingstoke, Palgrave Macmillan.

Human connection

In addition to my, *Effective Communication* book (3rd edn, Palgrave, 2018) and *People Skills*, useful resources in relation to this are:

Howe, D. (2008) *The Emotionally Intelligent Social Worker*, Basingstoke, Palgrave macmillan.

Moss, B. (2017) *Communication Skills in Health and Social Care*, 4th edn, London, Sage.

Smith, H. and Smith, M. K. (2008) *The Art of Helping Others: Being Around, Being There, Being Wise*, London, Jessica Kingsley Publishers.

In addition, one of the e-courses I have produced discusses emotional intelligence: *Emotional Competence: Developing Emotional Intelligence and Resilience* (see below for details).

Working with families

A useful starting point is Taibbi's chapter on family therapy in *Social Work Theory and Methods: The Essentials*. Other interesting material is to be found in:

Dallos, R. and Draper, R. (2015) *An Introduction to Family Therapy: Systemic Theory and Practice*, Maidenhead, Open University Press.

Reiter, M. D. (2017) *Family Therapy: An Introduction to Process, Practice and Theory*, New York, Routledge.

Working with groups

Mark Doel's work on groupwork is exemplary in its clarity and usefulness. You would do well to start with his chapter in *Social Work Theory and Methods: The Essentials* and then move on to his other work, such as:

Doel, M. (2006) *Using Groupwork*, London: Routledge/Community Care.

Doel, M. and Kelly, T. (2014) *A-Z Groups and Groupwork*, Basingstoke, Palgrave Macmillan.

Another helpful book is:

Gitterman, A. and Salmon, R. (eds) (2009) *Encyclopaedia of Social Work with Groups*, New York, Routledge.

Working with communities

There is a useful chapter on this by Paul Stepney in *Social Work Theory and Methods: The Essentials*. Stepney's other work is also useful:

Stepney, P. and Popple, K. (2008) *Social Work and the Community: A Critical Context for Practice*, Basingstoke, Palgrave Macmillan.

Another interesting text is:

Craig, G., Mayo, M., Popple, K., Shaw, M. and Taylor, M. (2011) *The Community Development Reader: History, Themes and Issues*, Bristol, The Policy Press.

Residential work

For this topic I would recommend:

Barton, S., Gonzalez, R. and Tomlinson, P. (2012) *Therapeutic Residential Care for Children and Young People*, London, Jessica Kingsley Publishers.

Johnson, J., Rolph, S. and Smith, R. (2010) *Residential Care: Transforming the Last Refuge*, Basingstoke, Palgrave Macmillan.

Smith, M., Fulcher, L. and Doran, P. (2013) *Residential Child Care in Practice: Making a Difference*, Bristol, The Policy Press.

Court work

You can find out more about court work by exploring what is on offer in:

Cooper, C. (2014) *Court and Legal Skills*, London, Palgrave.

Pollack, D. and Kleinman, T. G. (2015) *Social Work and the Courts*: *A Casebook*, 3rd edn, London, Routledge.

Seymour, C. and Seymour, R. (2011) *Courtroom and Report Writing Skills for Social Workers*, Exeter, Learning Matters.

Report writing and record keeping

My *Effective Communication* book (3rd edn, Palgrave, 2018) and my *Effective Writing* e-book will be of value in this regard, as will:

Moss, B. (2017) *Communication Skills in Health and Social Care*, 4th edn, London, Sage.

Pritchard, J. with Leslie, S. (2011) *Recording Skills in Safeguarding Adults: Best Practice and Evidential Requirements*, London, Jessica Kingsley Publishers.

Managing conflict

Conflict management has a large literature base, including:

Coleman, P. T. and Ferguson, R. (2014) *Making Conflict Work*, London, Piatkus.

Doherty, N. and Guyler, M. (2008) *The Essential Guide to Workplace Mediation and Conflict Resolution*, London, Kogan Page.

One of the e-courses I have developed is on the subject of *Handling Aggression* (see below).

Loss, grief and trauma

I have written extensively on the subject of loss and grief. A good starting point for further learning is my *Grief and its Challenges* book (Palgrave Macmillan, 2012). Other important texts include:

Corr, C., Corr, D. and Doka, K. J. (2017) *Death & Dying, Life & Living*, 8th edn, Boston, MA, Cengage.

Despelder, L. A. and Strickland, A. L. (2014) *The Last Dance: Encountering Death and Dying*, 10th edn, New York, McGraw-Hill.

Neimeyer, R. A., Harris, D. L., Winokuer, H. R. and Thornton, G. F. (eds) (2011) *Grief and Bereavement in Contemporary Society*, New York, Routledge.

Risk and decision making

Important material on risk is to be found in:

Kemshall, H., Wilkinson, B. and Baker, K. (2013) *Working with Risk: Skills for Contemporary Social Work*, Cambridge, Polity.

Webb, S. A. (2006) *Social Work in a Risk Society: Social and Political Perspectives*, Basingstoke, Palgrave Macmillan.

A good book on decision making in social work is:

O'Sullivan, T. (2011) *Decision Making in Social Work*, 2nd edn, Basingstoke, Palgrave Macmillan.

Also, one of my e-courses is on *Risk Assessment and Management* (see below).

Focusing on outcomes

Systematic practice is discussed in both *People Skills* and *Understanding Social Work*. My e-course on *Outcome-focused Practice* is also directly relevant.

Handling dilemmas and tensions

Dilemmas and tensions in social work are normally discussed in the literature on values and ethics, so, if this is an area you are particularly interested in, focusing on values and ethics would be your best start.

Handling criticism

Ray Jones's important book on social work and the media stands out as a key text in this area:

Jones, R. (2014) *The Story of Baby P: Setting the Record Straight*, Bristol, The Policy Press.

Complaints Panels in Social Care by Catherine Williams and Katy Ferris (Russell House, 2010) offers an interesting perspective on complaints.

Another important text is:

Doel, M. and Best, L. (2008), *Experiencing Social Work: learning from service users,* London: Sage.

Pitfalls to avoid

Emotional intelligence and resilience are covered in my e-course: *Emotional Competence: Developing Emotional Intelligence and Resilience.* Avoiding becoming a culture victim is discussed in *The Professional Social Worker*, while consumerism is covered in both *The Professional Social Worker* and *Social Problems and Social Justice*, as well as in the e-course, *Outcome-focused Practice.*

Surviving and thriving

My e-book *Stress Matters* (Avenue Media Solutions, 2015) provides a solid grounding in how to keep pressures within manageable limits and thereby avoid stress. My e-courses, *Dealing with Stress* and *Time and Workload Management* should also be helpful in this regard.

Managing your placement experience

Mark Doel's work is once again of value:

Doel, M. (2009) *Social Work Placements: A Traveller's Guide*, London, Routledge.

Surviving your Social Work Placement by Robert Lomax and Karen Jones (2nd edn, Palgrave, 2014) is also of interest. My e-course, *Learning to Learn*, should also help to make your placement a success.

Managing your career

The *Learning to Learn* e-course should also be useful in this regard. Beyond this, it is a matter of continuously looking for opportunities to keep developing.

Keeping the learning going

A good resource for getting the support you need to keep learning is:

Clutterbuck, D. (2014) *Everyone Needs a Mentor*, 2nd edn, London, Kogan Page.

And once again the *Learning to Learn* e-course should prove useful.

References

Brechin, A. (1993) 'Introducing Critical Practice', in Brechin *et al.* (1983).

Brechin, A., Brown, H. and Eby, M. A. (eds) (1983) *Critical Practice in Health and Social Care*, London, Sage.

Buber, M. (2004) *I and Thou*, 2nd edn, London, Continuum (German original 1923).

Desai, S. (2018) 'Solution-focused Practice', in Thompson and Stepney (2018).

Doka, K. J. (ed.) (1989) *Disenfranchised Grief: Recognizing Hidden Sorrow*, San Francisco, CA, Jossey Bass.

Doka, K. J. (2017) 'Disenfranchised Grief and Trauma', in Thompson *et al.* (2017).

England, H. (1986) *Social Work as Art: Making Sense for Good Practice*, London, HarperCollins.

Harms, L. (2018) 'Narrative Approaches', in Thompson and Stepney (2018).

Holloway, R. (2004) *Looking in the Distance: The Human Search for Meaning*, Edinburgh, Canongate.

Jones, R. (2014) *The Story of Baby P: Setting the Record Straight*, Bristol, The Policy Press.

Jordan, B. (2007) *Social Work and Well-being*, Lyme Regis, Russell House Publishing.

Mönnink, H. de (2017) *The Social Workers' Toolbox: Sustainable Multimethod Social Work,* London, Routledge.

Mooney, A. and Evans, B. (2015) *Language, Society and Power: An Introduction*, 4th edn, Abingdon, Routledge.

Neimeyer, R. A. (ed.) (2001) *Meaning Reconstruction and the Experience of Loss*, Washington DC, American Psychological Association.

Pink, D. H. (2011) *Drive: The Surprising Truth about What Motivates Us*, Edinburgh, Canongate Books.

Santayana, G. (2013) *The Life of Reason or The Phases of Human Progress*, Cambridge, MA, MIT Press.

Taibbi, R. (2018) 'Family Therapy', in Thompson and Stepney (2018).

Thompson, N. (2007) *Power and Empowerment*, Lyme Regis, Russell House Publishers.

Thompson, N. (2012a) *The People Solutions Sourcebook*, 2nd edn, Basingstoke, Palgrave Macmillan.

Thompson, N. (2012b) *Grief and its Challenges*, Basingstoke, Palgrave Macmillan.

Thompson, N. (2013) *People Management*, Basingstoke, Palgrave Macmillan.

Thompson, N. (2015a) *Understanding Social Work: Preparing for Practice*, 4th edn, London, Palgrave.

Thompson, N. (2015b) *People Skills*, 4th edn, London, Palgrave.

Thompson, N. (2015) *Stress Matters*, an e-book published by Avenue Media Solutions.

Thompson, N. (2016a) *A Career in Social Work*, an e-book published by Avenue Media Solutions.

Thompson, N. (2016b) *The Authentic Leader*, London, Palgrave.

Thompson, N. (2016c) *The Professional Social Worker*, 2nd edn, London, Palgrave.

Thompson, N. (2016d) *Anti-discriminatory Practice*, 6th edn, London, Palgrave.

Thompson, N. (2017a) *Theorizing Practice*, 2nd edn, London, Palgrave.

Thompson, N. (2017b) *Social Problems and Social Justice*, London, Palgrave.

Thompson, N. (2018a) *Promoting Equality: Working with Diversity and Difference*, 4th edn, London, Palgrave.

Thompson, N. (2018b) *Effective Communication: A Guide for the People Professions*, 3rd edn, London, Palgrave.

Thompson, N. (2018c) *Applied Sociology*, New York, Routledge.

Thompson, N. and Cox, G. (eds) (2017) *Handbook of the Sociology of Death, Grief, and Bereavement*, New York, Routledge.

Thompson, N., Cox, G and Stevenson, R. (eds) (2017) *Handbook of Traumatic Loss*, New York, Routledge.

Thompson, N. and Stepney, P. (eds) (2018) *Social Work Theory and Methods: The Essentials*, New York, Routledge.

Thompson, S. and Thompson, N. (2018) *The Critically Reflective Practitioner*, 2nd edn, London, Palgrave.

Learn with Neil

In my career spanning over 40 years a major focus of my work has been helping people to learn. In this final section of the manual I therefore present an overview of how I continue to help people learn – through my books and e-books, e-courses and my online learning community.

Books

The most relevant books of mine are the following:

Understanding Social Work (4th edition, Palgrave, 2015)

This book was written as a first step to a career in social work. It was developed for people considering a career in social work; people in the early stages of such a career; and for 'old hands' who want to revisit their roots.

The Social Work Companion (with Sue Thompson, 2nd edition, Palgrave, 2016)

Sue and I collaborated on this to put together a basic foundation of knowledge for social work students and practitioners. Of course, no book will tell you all you need to know, but this one will give you a solid foundation on which to build.

The Professional Social Worker: Meeting the Challenge (2nd edn, Palgrave, 2016)

This was written as a follow up to *Understanding Social Work*. It argues the case for reaffirming professionalism in social work and provides a detailed account of what good professional practice should involve.

People Skills (4th edn, Palgrave, 2015)

One of my most popular texts, this book explores three sets of essential skills: self-management skills; interaction skills; and intervention skills.

The People Solutions Sourcebook (2nd edn, Palgrave Macmillan, 2012)

This book comprises an extended essay on the problem-solving work that underpins social work and a discussion of 88 problem-solving tools. It has been very pleasing to get so much positive feedback from people who have told me they have found the tools really helpful in practice, whether on placement or after qualifying.

Anti-discriminatory Practice: Equality, Diversity and Social Justice (6th edn, Palgrave, 2016)

This has proven to be a very influential book, widely used by not only social workers, but also youth and community workers, probation officers, nurses, counsellors and various others. It establishes the foundations for making sure that we are challenging discrimination and oppression wherever possible.

Promoting Equality: Working with Diversity and Difference (4th edn, Palgrave, 2018)

Anti-discriminatory Practice provides a basic introduction to these important issues; it lays a foundation. This book then explores the issues in more depth and builds on that foundation.

Grief and its Challenges (Palgrave Macmillan, 2012)

Something that I have been aware of since the very early days of my career is that, wherever you are in social work, you are never far away from loss and grief, even though their effects will often be missed. This book therefore explains the significance of grief, as it applies across all sectors of social work, not just when someone has died.

Theorizing Practice (2nd edn, Palgrave, 2017)

The traditional idea is that we 'apply theory to practice'. This book argues that it is wiser to look at it the other way round, to begin with practice and then to draw on our professional knowledge base in accordance with the particular circumstances. That is what is meant by 'Theorizing practice'.

Social Problems and Social Justice (Palgrave, 2017)

Social work is part of a wider concern with social problems and with social justice. This book gives a picture of the background of social problems and social justice of which social work forms a part.

Applied Sociology (Routledge, 2018)

Effective social work practice involves being able to think critically and holistically. This book shows how sociological insights can be used to develop well-informed practice.

The Critically Reflective Practitioner (with Sue Thompson, 2nd edn, Palgrave, 2018)

Critically reflective practice is at the heart of good practice, but a lot of people are confused by what it actually means in practice. That is why we collaborated on this book to provide a clear picture of the theory in Part One and the practice in Part Two.

Social Work Theory and Methods: The Essentials (co-edited with Paul Stepney, Routledge, 2018)

A fresh look at social work theory and methods, with chapters on specific approaches contributed by a range of highly experienced experts.

E-books

I have also been involved in developing a range of e-books, including the following:

A Career in Social Work

This short e-book is in two parts. Part One tells the story of my own career in social work and then in Part Two there is a discussion of what a career in social work involves.

How to Do Social Work

This is another short e-book. It provides a basic overview of what is needed for effective practice,

Stress Matters

Social work is a highly pressurized job, and so the danger of stress is ever-present. This book challenges conventional notions of stress and emphasizes the importance of support, formal and informal.

Effective Writing

This is a basic guide to communicating effectively in writing. The skills involved are essential for all social workers.

Effective Teamwork: Developing Successful Teams

Positive teamwork can make a huge difference to quality of practice, job satisfaction and learning and development. This guide discusses what is involved in developing effective teamwork.

All the above are published by Avenue Media Solutions and are available from www.avenuemediasolution.com/shop or via other e-book retailers.

E-courses

I have developed a number of e-learning courses that are directly or indirectly relevant to social work:

Time and Workload Management

This course explores what I call the 'four principles of time and workload management'. It was developed to help people develop the skills and strategies for managing a heavy workload and staying in control.

Dealing with Stress

The *Time and Workload Management* course is very helpful when it comes to keeping stress at bay, but this course offers further guidance n making sure our pressures stay within manageable limits.

Emotional Competence: Developing Emotional Intelligence and Resilience

Social work is an emotionally demanding profession, and so it is important to have a good understanding of emotional issues and appreciate the skills involved. That is precisely what this course covers.

Handling Aggression

Unfortunately some people become aggressive or even violent when faced with situations they find frustrating or difficult. This course shows how to recognize early warning signs, how to defuse situations and how to deal with the aftermath.

Risk Assessment and Management

As we have seen, risk is an important issue in social work, but if we approach it in too rigid or anxious a way, we can make matters worse. This course explains the importance of a balanced approach to risk and gives guidance on how to achieve it.

Outcome-focused Practice

Unfocused practice where people allow situations to drift are not helpful to anyone. A systematic approach that is clear to everyone what the purpose of social work involvement is offers a much wiser approach, as this course makes clear.

Protecting Children from Abuse

Recognizing abuse, using the 'Follow the CROWD' approach and knowing what to do if abuse does arise are the two main topics covered by this course. Essential training for anyone who works with children.

Communicating with Children (with Mary Walsh)

Renowned child care expert, Mary Walsh, gives us the benefit of her experience and expertise in relation to communicating with children, with a clear focus on child-centred practice.

Childhood Trauma and Recovery (with Mary Walsh)

Mary has literally decades of experience of working with children who have been traumatized by abuse. In this course she shares that experience with us, so that we can have a better understanding of the issues involved.

Sexual Abuse and Childhood Sexuality (with Mary Walsh)

In this third and final part of the Mary Walsh trilogy, Mary explores the complex and difficult territory of sexual abuse and considers it from the point of view of childhood sexuality. This course provides an invaluable foundation of understanding.

The courses are hosted by the Avenue Learning Centre at www.avenuemediasolutions.com/shop.

The Avenue Professional Development Programme

This is a subscription-based online learning community based on principles of self-directed learning and geared towards promoting reflective practice.

Members of the Programme have access to:

- Online discussion forums that I contribute to, so a sort of online tutorial group.
- A growing library of multimedia learning resources; a new resource is added each month.
- A 12-part flexible structure, involving six learning themes and six learning domains (see below).
- Two e-books, one to plot your own learning pathway and one to review that pathway every three to six months.
- An e-portfolio for you to record and consolidate your learning.
- A 'Learning to Learn' e-course.
- A Grapevine facility with newsfeeds, blog feeds and Twitter feeds to help you keep up to date.
- A 'wiki' mini-encyclopaedia that members can contribute to.
- An online 'Coffee Shop' for members to chat and get to know one another.

The 12-part structure is based on six learning themes:

Self-management ▲ **I**nteraction skills ▲ **L**eadership ▲ **V**alues-based practice ▲ **E**mpowerment ▲ **R**apport building and networking

and six learning domains:

Professionalism ▲ **L**earning and development ▲ **A**iming higher ▲ **C**ompetent practice ▲ **E**mployee well-being ▲ **S**pirituality

Further information is available from:

www.apdp.org.uk.

Connect with Neil on social media

I have a strong online presence, so feel free to connect with me online:

humansolutions website and newsletter: www.humansolutions.org.uk.

Facebook page: https://www.facebook.com/drneilthompson/.

Facebook group: Social Work Focus

https://www.facebook.com/groups/1640523002636327/

LinkedIn: https://www.linkedin.com/in/drneilthompson/.

Twitter: @drneilthompson

Learn with Neil Thompson YouTube channel:
https://www.youtube.com/channel/UC7UWHGrxszahkLfCJgCgtYw.

Blog and website: www.NeilThompson.info.

Printed in Great Britain
by Amazon